More Praise for
# The Little Book of Main Street Money

"Jonathan Clements is one of those rare financial writers who is thought-provoking, sensible, informed, and insightful. This new book is his best yet!"

Eric Tyson, author of
*Personal Finance For Dummies*

"Personal finance books are a dime a dozen, but this one is a gold mine. Jonathan Clements has taken his must-read *Wall Street Journal* columns and distilled them into the simple truths that help real people make real money."

Consuelo Mack, anchor,
Consuelo Mack WealthTrack

"Jonathan Clements is one of the best personal finance writers of our time. He has crafted a pithy primer to help us navigate stormy seas. Those who care about their happiness, ignore it at their own peril."

Terry Burnham, Ph.D., author of
*Mean Markets and Lizard Brains*

# THE LITTLE BOOK
# OF
# MAIN STREET
# MONEY

# Little Book Big Profits Series

In the *Little Book Big Profits* series, the brightest icons in the financial world write on topics that range from tried-and-true investment strategies to tomorrow's new trends. Each book offers a unique perspective on investing, allowing the reader to pick and choose from the very best in investment advice today.

Books in the *Little Book Big Profits* series include:

*The Little Book That Beats the Market,* in which Joel Greenblatt, founder and managing partner at Gotham Capital, reveals a "magic formula" that is easy to use and makes buying good companies at bargain prices automatic, enabling you to successfully beat the market and professional managers by a wide margin.

*The Little Book of Value Investing,* in which Christopher Browne, managing director of Tweedy, Browne Company, LLC, the oldest value investing firm on Wall Street, simply and succinctly explains how value investing, one of the most effective investment strategies ever created, works, and shows you how it can be applied globally.

*The Little Book of Common Sense Investing,* in which Vanguard Group founder John C. Bogle shares his own time-tested philosophies, lessons, and personal anecdotes to explain why outperforming the market is an investor illusion, and how the simplest of investment strategies—indexing—can deliver the greatest return to the greatest number of investors.

*The Little Book That Makes You Rich,* in which Louis Navellier, financial analyst and editor of investment newsletters since 1980, offers readers a fundamental understanding of how to get rich using the best in growth-investing strategies. Filled with in-depth insights and practical advice, *The Little Book That Makes You Rich* outlines an effective approach to building true wealth in today's markets.

*The Little Book That Builds Wealth,* in which Pat Dorsey, director of stock analysis for leading independent investment research provider Morningstar, Inc., guides the reader in understanding "economic moats," learning how to measure them against one another, and selecting the best companies for the very best returns.

*The Little Book That Saves Your Assets,* in which David M. Darst, a managing director of Morgan Stanley, who chairs the firm's Global Wealth Management Asset Allocation and Investment Policy Committee, explains the role of asset allocation in maximizing investment returns to meet life objectives. Brimming with the wisdom gained from years of practical experience, this book is a vital road map to a secure financial future.

*The Little Book of Bull Moves in Bear Markets,* in which Peter D. Schiff, President of Euro Pacific Capital, Inc., looks at historical downturns in the financial markets to analyze what investment strategies succeeded and shows how to implement various bull moves so that readers can preserve, and even enhance, their wealth within a prosperous or an ailing economy.

*The Little Book of Main Street Money*, in which Jonathan Clements, award-winning columnist for the *Wall Street Journal* and a director of the new personal finance service myFi, offers 21 commonsense truths about investing to help readers take control of their financial futures.

# THE LITTLE BOOK

## OF

# MAIN STREET MONEY

*21 Simple Truths that Help Real*
*People Make Real Money*

# JONATHAN CLEMENTS

**WILEY**

John Wiley & Sons, Inc.

Published by John Wiley & Sons, Inc., Hoboken, New Jersey.
Published simultaneously in Canada.

For general information on our other products and services or for technical support, please contact our Customer Care Department within the United States at (800) 762-2974, outside the United States at (317) 572-3993 or fax (317) 572-4002.

Wiley also publishes its books in a variety of electronic formats. Some content that appears in print may not be available in electronic books. For more information about Wiley products, visit our web site at www.wiley.com.

*Library of Congress Cataloging-in-Publication Data*

Clements, Jonathan.
    The little book of main street money : 21 simple truths that help real people make real money / Jonathan Clements.
        p.   cm. — (Little book big profits series)
    ISBN 978-0-470-47323-8 (cloth)
        1. Investments.   2. Portfolio management.   3. Finance, Personal.   I. Title.
HG4521.C514   2009
332.6—dc22

                                                                                    2009007445

Printed in the United States of America.

10   9   8   7   6   5   4   3   2   1

*For Carolyn*

# Contents

Chapter Four
Even the Best Investors Need
to Be Great Savers

Chapter Five
Time Is as Valuable as Money

Chapter Six
No Investment Is Risk-Free

Chapter Seven
Portfolio Performance: It's All in the Mix

Chapter Eight
Stocks Are Worth *Something*

Chapter Nine
To Add Wealth, We Need to Overcome
the Subtractions

Chapter Ten
Aiming for Average Is the Only
Sure Way to Win

# Foreword

———— ∾ ————

JONATHAN SURE PICKED A HELL of a time to write a personal finance book. With 2008—the worst year for stocks since 1931—just behind us, about the last thing most people want to read about is how to manage what little money they have left. And yet investors ignore *The Little Book of Main Street Money* at their peril, for two reasons.

First, future stock returns, by any conventional yardstick, should be quite agreeable from this point forward. How is this possible, given the horrible state of the global economy and its increasingly creaky financial system? Simple. Thanks to the shellacking of 2008 and early 2009, stocks around the world have already borne their brunt. Along the way, they exhibited a degree of volatility not seen since the Great Depression. Between July and

December 2008, for example, one index of real estate investment trusts (REITs) moved up or down more than 5 percent on 45 trading days, more than 10 percent on 16 days, and more than 15 percent on three days.

According to the perverse logic of the markets, prices *had* to fall to the point where investors could be assured that they would be rewarded for bearing high economic risk and extreme financial volatility. In the United States, yields now stand at almost 4 percent for the Standard & Poor's 500, 5 percent for unglamorous value stocks and 11 percent for REITs. Abroad, the yields—and thus expected future returns—are even fatter. In other words, high risk and high returns go hand in hand. Truly, the best fishing is usually done in the most troubled waters. If there were ever a time to gather your financial wits about you, it is now.

Second, with a quarter-century of journalistic experience and more than a thousand *Wall Street Journal* personal finance columns under his belt, you've just picked the best wit-gatherer in the business. What makes Jonathan's perspectives unique is not just his depth of experience or intellectual bona fides. Yes, *Forbes* and the *Wall Street Journal* tend not to hire dummies, and going further back, Cambridge University's student newspaper knew what it was doing when it made him editor. Rather, he is one of the best *listeners* in the business. Anyone can be taught by financial experts, but Jonathan, more than almost all of his colleagues, has learned from the experiences of his readers.

So don't be fooled by the fact that this is, well, a little book. You'll find more pearls per page between its covers than in almost any other financial title. So comprehensive, in fact, is *The Little Book of Main Street Money* that I found it more than a little challenging to add much to it in this foreword.

After some thought, I came up with one thing that readers should always keep in the back of their minds when reading even the very best of finance books: The name of the investing game is not to get rich, but rather to not get poor. Rest assured, these are not the same thing.

Over three centuries ago, the famous French philosopher Blaise Pascal defended his belief in God in the following manner: Suppose that the Almighty does not in fact exist. The atheist wins and the believer loses. If God does exist, the situation reverses.

The consequences of being wrong with each belief, however, are starkly different. If a supreme being doesn't exist, then all the devout has lost is the opportunity to fornicate, imbibe, and skip a lot of dull church services. But if God does exist, then the atheist roasts eternally in Hell. The rational person—or, at a minimum, someone who believes that God actually cares how he behaves and what he thinks—thus chooses to believe in Him.

But for the moment, at least, both Jonathan and I believe in something else entirely: that in the coming decades the Almighty will provide mighty rewards to long-term stock investors. You might think that this means that we favor 100 percent stock portfolios. But you'd be mistaken.

You see, when you invest, you are squarely in Pascal's Wager territory. *You could be wrong.* Start by imagining that Jonathan and I are right, and that stocks do in fact deliver boffo returns over the coming decades. Furthermore, imagine that, in spite of this, you've invested conservatively, with stock exposure of less than 60 percent. Clearly, you'll make less money—a good deal less—than had you gone a more aggressive route. The consequences of this "mistake"? You'll be driving a Camry in retirement, instead of a Lexus, and vacationing in Miami, rather than in Tahiti. Disappointing, but hardly disastrous.

Now, consider what happens in the opposite situation, namely, Jonathan and I are wrong about high equity returns and you go flat out on stocks. Say we're *disastrously* wrong and stocks lose more than 90 percent of their value, as they did between 1929 and 1932. Clearly, the consequences of this mistake—no quote marks needed—would be far, far worse. Sure, the 40 percent or more of bonds you're left with also won't pay for the Lexus and Tahiti, but at least you won't be a burden on your relatives or subsisting on an Alpo diet. Remember, the name of the game isn't to get rich; it's to not become poor. (In fact, anyone owning a solid dollop of bonds during the Great Depression was more than grateful for them. Not only did they collect a decent coupon, but also the purchasing power of their principal and interest went a lot further, thanks to prolonged deflation.)

Reaching for higher returns has sent many an investor to the poorhouse. Think about it: If you have a single dollar and you wanted to get rich, your best—and only—shot is to buy a lottery ticket. No one in his right mind, however, would make this the cornerstone of his investment policy.

By the same token, you'll hear—often from reputable sources—that you should limit your stock picks to a few well-chosen names, so as to maximize your returns. Hogwash! Pascal's Wager again: *What are the consequences of being wrong with such a concentrated bet?* A list of 5 or 10 stocks—even one chosen by the best money managers—is as likely to become an all-clunker portfolio as the ticket to riches.

So yes, like a lottery ticket, a small, focused portfolio *does* maximize your chances of getting rich. Unfortunately, it also maximizes your chances of dying poor. By contrast, the worst that can happen to you with a 60/40 portfolio, in which the stock portion is spread prudently and widely around the investment universe, should be a loss in the 30 to 35 percent range. Bad news, to be sure, but not as catastrophic as taking an unlucky draw of a handful of names and adding it to a bear market.

Over the past quarter-century, a thousand *Wall Street Journal* columns, and tens of thousands of e-mails and letters from readers, Jonathan has become one of the world's great connoisseurs of the myriad ways in which people become unnecessarily poor. *The Little Book of Main Street Money* is nothing if not a compendium of these financial neck breakers and a roadmap around them. So sit back, relax, and allow Jonathan Clements—and Blaise Pascal— to show you how to win by not losing.

—WILLIAM BERNSTEIN
Author, *The Four Pillars of Investing*
March 2009

# Introduction

## *Let the Rebuilding Begin*

IT MAY BE A SHOTGUN WEDDING. But trust me, you and Wall Street could learn to love each other.

In 2008 and 2009, we have been hit with what is arguably the worst financial debacle since the Great Depression of the 1930s—a devastating mix of plunging share prices, crippling consumer debts, slumping home prices, and rising unemployment. And things weren't exactly hunky-dory to begin with. Consider the financial backdrop. In recent decades, traditional company pensions have been disappearing. Retirements have grown longer and hence more expensive. Financial choices have become more befuddling. Job security has faded. College costs have soared.

What to do? We don't have much choice: We need to seize control of our financial lives, embrace the markets, and be smarter about money than ever before. For most of us, this is a daunting proposition. Wall Street is tough to love. Markets skyrocket one moment, plunge the next. The lingo is baffling. The complexity can be mind-boggling. And the stakes are huge. Feeling nervous? Fret not. If we can keep some simple truths in mind, we could make this marriage work.

In fact, a firm grip on financial basics has rarely been more important. This is a moment of extraordinary doubt—about the stock market, about the housing market, about the economy, about our future prosperity. But we have recovered from worse and we will recover from this. To rebuild our finances, we need to cast aside yesterday's fanciful thinking and profligate ways, and get back to first principles. Don't let today's economic mayhem distract you: The value of time-tested financial truths still endures.

This *Little Book* may run a modest 36,000 words and writing it may have taken just a fistful of months. Yet, to me, it represents a lifetime of work, pulling together the many ideas I have wrestled with and advocated during my quarter-century watching Wall Street and writing about money. Eighteen of those years were spent at the *Wall Street Journal*, where—as the newspaper's personal finance columnist—I tried to help regular investors make sense of their finances. More recently, I have endeavored to do the same as Director of Financial Guidance for myFi (www .myFi.com), short for "my financial life," a new financial service from Citicorp that's geared toward everyday Americans.

This book, however, is more than just a compendium of useful financial ideas, though there are plenty of those in the chapters that follow. Rather, it reflects the financial philosophy I've developed over the years. The tax rates, historical returns, and other gory financial details mentioned in these pages will soon be out of date. But I hope the philosophy espoused here—the way of thinking about financial issues—will have lasting value.

That philosophy encompasses seven key beliefs I have harped on again and again during my career.

1. *Money is a means to an end.* It isn't an end in itself. Before we buy a mutual fund or purchase an insurance policy, we need to figure out why we're amassing money and what we are looking to protect. If we don't know what our goals are, we may not settle on the right strategy and we'll be less inclined to make the necessary sacrifices.

2. *We shouldn't neglect today.* We're often encouraged to save for distant goals, like our toddler's college education and our own retirement. But this is an awfully long time to wait for financial nirvana. My

advice: Also strive for peace of mind today. That means getting our debts under control, living comfortably within our paycheck, ensuring we have the right insurance, devising a plan for financial emergencies, and spending our money on the things that matter most to us. Indeed, if we take care of today, we will likely find we are also taking care of tomorrow.

3. *We need to think harder about what we want.* We imagine that our lives will be somehow transformed if we win that next promotion or we buy the bigger house. But even when we get our heart's desire, eternal satisfaction eludes us. As we take care of today and prepare for tomorrow, we need to think much harder about how we spend our money and how we spend our time.

4. *Money is emotional.* We struggle to save regularly and we find it difficult to invest rationally. There's the prudent, unemotional strategy. And then there's the plan that we can live with. If we're going to be contented stewards of our money, we need to settle on strategies that will get us to our goals—and that we'll stick with along the way.

5. *Our financial lives are bigger than we think.* Managing money isn't just about our stocks, bonds, and mutual funds. There are also our debts, our homes, our financial promises to our children, our income-earning

ability, and so much more. To handle our finances wisely, we need to consider the whole as well as the parts, so we can make key tradeoffs, spot opportunities, and figure out what's missing.

6. *We should focus on the things we can control.* We may not be able to influence the inflation rate, the direction of bond yields, or what happens to stock prices. But there's much we can control, including how much we save and spend, how much we pay in investment costs and taxes, how much investment risk we take, and how we react to the markets' ups and downs. My suggestion: Let's stop worrying about the things we can't control and focus on the things we can. This is a humbler approach to managing money—and yet one that's often more rewarding.

7. *Simplicity is one of the great financial virtues.* Most of us may never understand credit default swaps, commodities backwardation, and mortgage derivatives, but we don't have to. It's possible to make good money using straightforward strategies and plain vanilla mutual funds. In fact, simpler is usually better, because it will often involve lower costs and less chance for foolishness. Moreover, if we stick with simple strategies and simple investments, we will likely understand what we own—and that should make us more tenacious when we're tested by turbulent markets.

These seven points guide my thinking, influence my own finances, and infuse the pages that follow. Everybody's financial situation is a little different and the specific suggestions offered in the next 21 chapters may not be right for you. Before you make any decisions, you'll want to consider a host of factors, including your stomach for risk, your goals, your income, your nest egg's size, and your tax bracket. Still, whether you invest on your own or you rely on a team of financial advisers, I hope the philosophy and financial principles advocated here will help you better manage your money.

In the spirit of the *Little Book* series, I have tried to keep this book short, so that it is accessible to even the most financially phobic. With any luck, you will like what you read and you'll want to share this book with your friends, neighbors, siblings, and—maybe most important—your adult children. As I wrote each chapter, I often thought about the ideas I want to pass along to my children, Hannah and Henry, who are on cusp of the adult world. To make those ideas easy to digest and easy to understand, I have attempted to cut out all verbal flabbiness, distill my thinking down to some key notions, and express myself as succinctly and clearly as possible. I can't promise to have achieved those goals. But I tried mightily.

# Chapter One

# Our Finances Are Bigger than a Brokerage Account

*Pondering the Paycheck
in the Mirror*

THINK BIG. Really big.

Ask folks about their financial lives and they might mention their 401(k) retirement savings plan, their bank accounts, and their mortgage. But in truth, our financial lives are far, far larger. How large? Wrap your brain around these four contentions:

1. The retired teachers around the corner shouldn't have nearly so much in bonds, and certainly far less than the retired lawyers who live next door.
2. Your penniless 22-year-old niece is a millionaire and she should diversify by investing heavily in stocks.
3. Your real estate agent may be super-savvy when it comes to the property market, but that doesn't mean she should buy rental real estate.
4. Your brother-in-law is betting on stocks with borrowed money and he doesn't even know it.

Puzzled? To understand what's at issue here, consider everything you own—and everything you owe.

## Taking Stock

As you tote up your assets, your thoughts probably turn first to things like your savings account, individual stocks and bonds, mutual funds, and real estate. But don't stop there. You would also want to include your Social Security retirement benefit and any pension you're entitled to. When you and your spouse die, your Social Security and pension may cease to have any value. But while you're alive, these two assets are like enormous bonds, kicking off heaps of regular income. A fixed monthly pension is similar to a conventional fixed-interest bond, generating the same income every year. Meanwhile, Social Security, in its current form, is like owning a big inflation-indexed bond, delivering a stream of income that rises along with inflation.

That brings us to our retired teachers, who receive pensions for all of their years of service in the local school district. If those pensions cover much or all of their living expenses, they won't need much income from their conventional investment portfolio, thus freeing them up to invest more heavily in stocks. Stocks don't kick off as much income as bonds and they involve considerably more risk, but they also potentially deliver higher long-run returns.

In fact, investing heavily in stocks will diversify our retired teachers' bond-like pensions and it could salvage their standard of living later in retirement. The reason: If their pensions are fixed, the spending power of that monthly income will decline over time as inflation takes its toll. Later in retirement, they may find their pensions no longer cover all of their living expenses. But if they took the precaution of investing part of their portfolio in stocks and leaving it to grow, they may amass a handsome nest egg that'll help sustain their lifestyle in their later years.

By contrast, the retired lawyers next door aren't entitled to a pension. Instead, to cover their living expenses, they will need to rely on their savings and Social Security. To ensure they have a reasonably reliable stream of income, they might hold a fairly standard retirement portfolio, with maybe half their money in bonds and half in stocks. During their working years, the lawyers may have invested their savings more aggressively, with a hefty percentage stashed in stocks and only a modest sum in bonds. But back then, of course, they didn't need income from their portfolio, because they had regular paychecks coming in.

Think of these regular paychecks as the return on human capital, possibly the most overlooked asset. This is the reason your penniless 22-year-old niece can consider herself a millionaire. She is like an enormous bond that will likely generate income for the next four decades— a bond that might easily be worth $1 million. As your niece considers how to invest her savings, she doesn't need yet more income. Instead, what she needs is long-term growth, so that one day she can afford to retire. With that in mind, and also to diversify her big "bond" holding, your niece might invest heavily in stocks. But as she approaches retirement and the waning of her human capital, she'll probably want to follow the lead of the retired lawyers, cutting back on stocks and adding to her bonds. See Exhibit 1.1.

**EXHIBIT 1.1   You, Inc.**

*As you think about how much you're worth, here are some
assets and liabilities to consider.*

| Assets | Liabilities |
| --- | --- |
| Human capital | Paying for retirement |
| Home | Children's college |
| Stocks | Other goals |
| Bonds | Mortgage |
| Bank accounts | Student loans |
| Pension | Credit-card debt |
| Social Security | Auto loans |

Not everybody's paycheck is like a bond. If you're a
salesperson paid on commission, an employee of a financially troubled company, an actress who works sporadi-
cally, or an executive whose annual income varies widely
because of an unpredictable bonus, your income is less
bond-like and you may want to stash more of your savings
in bonds, certificates of deposit, money-market funds, and
other conservative investments. That will give you assets
that can be easily sold if your income proves lower than
expected.

Even if you're confident your job is secure and your
income will cover your living costs, and you are therefore
comfortable taking a fair amount of risk with your savings, you should think carefully about the type of risk you
take. For instance, your real estate agent may be inclined

to buy rental real estate, because she's well versed on the property market and she figures that that will give her an edge. Similarly, Silicon Valley workers might be tempted to invest in the hot new technology company they heard about, oil company employees might purchase energy shares, and almost everybody considers buying their employer's stock. Yes, some employees receive shares as part of their compensation. But many others choose to invest heavily in their company's stock. Buying what we know can be enormously comforting.

But in these examples, it might not be smart. What if the real estate market implodes, the technology sector craters, oil prices plunge, or our employer gets into financial trouble? In each situation, we're looking at a potential double whammy—both losing our jobs and losing our savings.

## Living with Leverage

To complement your new, expansive view of your assets, aim to adopt a similar approach to your liabilities. Your liabilities aren't just your mortgage, student loans, credit card balances, and auto loans. They also include the cost of your goals, such as buying that next car and paying for your children's college education.

Maybe more important, there is the cost of your retirement, which is the key reason you need to save and invest during your four decades in the workforce. I hate to reduce the broad sweep of our lives to a grim calculus involving dollars and cents. Still, from a purely economic perspective, our working years can be viewed as a period when we amass financial capital so that one day we can live without the income from our human capital. Your niece's income-earning ability may be worth more than $1 million. But that's just as well, because that seven-figure human capital will come in handy as she seeks to amass a seven-figure retirement portfolio.

Taking a broader view of your finances can bring some startling insights—and some ways to improve your finances. Remember your brother-in-law, who is investing in stocks with borrowed money and doesn't know it? We all engage in mental accounting, associating the mortgage with the house and the auto loan with the car. But once we have these debts, they leverage our entire finances. Let's say your brother-in-law has a $300,000 home, $150,000 in stock funds, and $50,000 in bonds and other conservative investments. Meanwhile, his debts include a $225,000 mortgage, a $20,000 car loan, and $5,000 in credit card debt. What he effectively has is $500,000 in real estate and investments, but half of it is bought with borrowed money, so his net worth is only $250,000.

This sort of leverage lets us own more stuff than we can currently afford. It works best when our investments earn returns that are higher than the interest rate we're paying on our borrowed money. But leverage can also bite when things go wrong, sharply worsening our losses. If your brother-in-law's bonds held steady at $50,000, but his home slipped in value to $240,000 and his stocks slumped to $110,000, his total assets would drop 20 percent from $500,000 to $400,000. That might seem grim. But what's really grim is the hit to his net worth, which would plunge 40 percent from $250,000 to $150,000.

Even without a market decline, leverage can sting. Your brother-in-law's bonds might be yielding 5 percent, while his credit cards could be costing 14 percent. The implication: Your brother-in-law should probably cash in $5,000 of his bonds and use it to pay off his credit card debt. That would reduce risk by trimming the amount he's borrowing and simultaneously save him money.

Indeed, bonds and borrowed money can be viewed as mirror opposites. One pays you interest. The other costs you interest. You might even think of borrowed money as a *negative bond*. Your brother-in-law may assume he is being pretty conservative, because he has $50,000 in bonds. But thanks to his $250,000 in debts, his net bond position is a negative $200,000 and he is forking over a lot more interest each month than he's earning.

That doesn't mean your brother-in-law is taking too much risk. After all, if he has a paycheck coming in, he may have no problem servicing his debts. But as your brother-in-law approaches retirement and considers buying more bonds in his portfolio, he should probably also look to pay off his debts. That way, when he retires and no longer has a salary coming in, he will be earning a lot more interest than he's paying.

---

### Street Smarts

- If you have a long time to retirement and a secure, steady salary, consider diversifying this bond-like income by buying stocks.
- Don't double risk by investing heavily in the economic sector that provides your paycheck.
- Borrowing allows you to own more stuff than you can currently afford—but it will exacerbate your losses during market downturns.

Chapter Two

# We Can't Have It All

### And That Means We Need to Make Tough Financial Choices

EVERYTHING'S A TRADEOFF.

If we take on the expensive car lease, we will have less for the summer vacation. If we opt to splurge on the summer vacation, we won't have as much for savings. If we decide to save like crazy for retirement and the kids' college education, we won't be able to buy as big a house.

Within reason, none of these choices is bad. But they are indeed choices—and yet often we give them scant thought. Instead, we haphazardly spend here and save there, without considering the implications for other areas of our financial life. In the previous chapter, we took the big-picture view of assets and liabilities. Now, it's time to take the same approach to spending and saving.

## Doling Out Dollars

As we decide how to divvy up our paychecks, we need to make three basic choices. First, we have to weigh purchasing one item versus purchasing another. Next, we need to weigh purchasing today versus saving for tomorrow. And finally, when saving for tomorrow, we have to decide what we'll save for.

All this may make it sound like we enjoy a world of possibilities. But that is hardly the case. A hefty portion of our paycheck is oftentimes already spoken for, claimed by essentials such as mortgage or rent, car payments, taxes, health care, utilities, and food. Once these have taken their bite, our room to maneuver is considerably smaller. To be sure, we can live beyond our means in the short term, by tapping our home's equity, racking up the credit cards, or borrowing in other ways. But that isn't sustainable. Over the long haul, we are constrained by our incomes—which is why it's so important to make conscious choices, rather than haphazardly doling out our hard-earned dollars.

As we dish out those dollars, we may need to cut corners. There's a daunting laundry list of good financial practices, including maxing out our employer's 401(k) retirement savings plan, fully funding an individual retirement account, stashing dollars in 529 college savings plans for our kids, buying a home, keeping an emergency reserve equal to six months of living expenses, and covering ourselves with a heap of insurance, including disability, health, life, long-term care, homeowner's, auto, and umbrella liability insurance.

Overwhelming? It certainly is. Most of us can't possibly afford to do it all, so we need to decide what's critical and what is merely desirable. Many folks have four basic goals: They want to buy a home, help the kids with college, pay for their own retirement, and make sure they are okay if they're hit with some sort of financial calamity.

This last goal is often the easiest area to cut back on. Blanket insurance coverage may be comforting, but it is also mighty expensive. We can often trim costs by raising a policy's deductibles or reducing its benefits. We may also get by with an emergency reserve equal to less than six months of living expenses if, say, we have easy access to borrowed money through a home equity line of credit. Carrying less insurance and holding less emergency money can make particular sense if you and your spouse both work. Even if one of you gets laid off or can't work because of an accident or illness, you may be able to squeak by on the other spouse's paycheck.

## Stiffing the Kids

After you've reined in the money you spend on protecting your family, the decisions get tougher. Do you go for the big house, pay for the kids' college, or fund your own retirement? I would argue that, if money is tight, it is no contest: Forget the big house, stiff the kids, and shovel those dollars into your 401(k).

I am not arguing that real estate is a lousy investment, that children ought to pay their own college costs or that there's virtue in financial selfishness. If you can afford to buy a big house and foot the bill for part or all of your children's tuition, that's great. But the fact is, you don't have to own a big house and you don't have to pay for the kids' college, but one day you will have to retire.

This might seem like an unnecessary tradeoff. Often, the temptation is to put off saving for retirement and instead deal with goals in the order they occur. That might mean buying the house in your thirties, paying for the children's college in your forties and then saving for retirement in your fifties. But financially, it makes sense to deal with goals concurrently rather than consecutively—and that means starting to save for retirement right away, while scaling back on the house and skimping on the college funding.

To understand why, suppose you are age 30. Your kids might be just 15 years from college, while your retirement could be 35 years away—and you might live another 25 years after that. The college bills may be a whole lot closer, but the time horizon for your retirement money is far, far longer. That means you can take greater risk by stashing more of your retirement nest egg in stocks, which should translate into higher long-run returns. In addition, with your retirement money, you may have the chance to fund an employer's 401(k) plan. No investment vehicle—not even a 529 college savings plan with its tax-free growth—can rival the financial benefits of a good 401(k). A traditional 401(k) plan will offer an initial tax deduction, tax-deferred growth, and possibly a matching employer contribution.

Moreover, if you don't start saving for retirement by your thirties, it can be awfully tough to amass enough by age 65. Imagine a world where you can earn a steady 5 percent a year. That might seem modest. But we're also assuming no inflation. In a world without rising consumer prices, 5 percent would be a pretty handsome rate of return. Indeed, at 5 percent a year, if you saved $400 a month starting at age 30, you would have $456,000 at age 65. What if you focus on other goals and don't get around to saving for retirement until age 40? Over the next 25 years, to amass the same $456,000, you would need to sock away more than $760 a month.

Getting an early jump on retirement savings doesn't just make the required savings rate less daunting. It also gives you options. When you are in your twenties and new to the work world, your job might seem wonderfully exciting and the prospect of working until age 65 might seem like no big deal. By your forties, the excitement may be long gone and you might be looking to go back to school or switch to a more stimulating but less lucrative career. If you have been saving diligently since your twenties, you will have those sorts of options. If you haven't, you are likely headed back to the office, possibly to a job you have come to loathe.

But what about the kids? If necessary, your children can always borrow to pay for college. In fact, there's a heap of financial assistance available to college students, including grant money and low-interest loans. By contrast, nobody will lend you money to pay for retirement, except maybe the local reverse-mortgage lender. Want to retire in comfort? You will to need to pony up cold, hard cash.

---

### Street Smarts

- Never forget that a dollar spent on one item is a dollar you can't devote to other desires.
- To make it easier to amass enough for retirement, aim to start saving no later than age 30.
- If money is tight, consider raising your insurance deductibles, keeping a smaller emergency reserve, purchasing a more modest home, and asking your kids to pay their own college expenses.

# Chapter Three

# Money Can Buy Happiness—If We Spend It Carefully

### Getting in Touch with Our Inner Caveman

WE WANT THE BIG HOUSE AND THE FANCY CAR. We hanker after the fat pay raise and the next promotion. And, because we aren't entirely consistent, we also hunger for a life of endless leisure.

Sound familiar? There's just one problem. While all of these things may briefly make us happy, none will buy us lasting happiness. Cast your mind back to the last chapter, about the need to make financial tradeoffs. If you have a sense you aren't making the right choices, there is a reason: We just aren't very good at figuring out what we want.

Much of this, I believe, has evolutionary roots. Unfortunately, we can't go back and interview our hunter-gatherer ancestors. But we can take a pretty good shot at imagining what their lives were like. These folks weren't focused on saving diligently so they could retire in 30 years. They were focused on surviving until tomorrow. That was no easy task. They strove relentlessly to feed and shelter themselves, they consumed whenever they could, and they weren't the type to lounge around their caves and muse, "I'm one lucky dude. In fact, I'm totally content with what I have and there's really nothing more I could possibly want."

We aren't so different.

## Making Progress

In recent decades, the U.S. standard of living has vastly improved. Yet people, on average, report being no more satisfied with their lives than they did in earlier decades. Money, it appears, hasn't bought much happiness. Why not?

Psychologists have posited the notion of the *hedonic treadmill* or *hedonic adaptation*. The idea: We strive to get that bigger house or that next promotion and, when we achieve these things, we are indeed briefly happy. But soon enough, the thrill wears off and we are lusting after something else. Like our cave-dwelling ancestors, we're never truly satisfied and we are always striving to get ahead.

Some have argued that what counts isn't our absolute standard of living, but rather our income and wealth relative to those around us. Sure enough, people who are better off are more likely to say they're happy. But this may be a *focusing illusion*. When assessed at different points during the day, those with higher incomes report suffering more anxiety and anger. But if you sit these folks down and ask them whether they're happy, they think about their lot in life and they realize they are relatively fortunate. They figure they ought to be happy—so that's what they say.

This doesn't mean money can't buy happiness. As people are lifted out of poverty and brought up to a fairly basic standard of living, their happiness can vastly increase. But after that, a lot of extra dollars don't necessarily buy a lot of extra happiness. We often find ourselves running on the hedonic treadmill, desperately pursuing happiness, but never making much progress.

How can we get ourselves off the treadmill and squeeze more happiness out of the dollars we have? We need to set aside conventional notions of what the good life is all about—and think much more carefully about how we spend our money and how we spend our time. On that score, here are six suggestions.

1. *Buy experiences, rather than things.*

When we consider what we would do with extra money, we typically imagine buying things—the new car, the bigger house, the latest gadget, the new clothes. The problem is, the thrill from these purchases doesn't just fade quickly. Worse still, these objects can turn into sources of unhappiness. The car gets scratched, the house needs a new roof, the gadget breaks, and the clothes begin to look worn. These items, which had so captivated us when we first bought them, eventually come to irritate and annoy us.

This is less likely to happen if we spend our money on experiences. Suppose we go out to dinner with friends, take the kids to the amusement park, or travel to Europe with the family. True, the money is soon gone, these experiences are quickly over, and nothing of tangible value remains. But that's an advantage. Unlike objects, such experiences don't grow old and become irksome. Instead, all we are left with are cherished memories. We may even sanitize those memories as the years go by, so our cherished memories become even more cherished.

2. *Count your blessings.*

The thrill from the new house, car, gadget, and clothes will soon wane. You will also quickly forget the latest promotion and the accompanying pay raise. Even the trip to Europe will eventually become a distant memory.

To counteract all of this, go out and celebrate the promotion, so you hang on to the good feelings for a little longer. Make sure you remember the trip to Europe by framing a few vacation photos and putting them up in the living room. Stop for a moment and admire your house. All of these things should slow the process of adaptation—and give you a little more happiness for your money and your efforts.

3. *Strive for a sense of control.*

We don't do very well with uncertainty. To be sure, some is inevitable. But some we inflict on ourselves. For instance, if buying the big house and the fancy car means borrowing a heap of money, we may suffer gnawing uncertainty, as we fret over whether we can make the next monthly debt payments. If the big house is in a distant suburb, we will also have the uncertainty of a long commute, never knowing how bad the traffic will be or how late the trains are running. Research suggests that commuting is terrible for happiness, often ranking as the worst part of our day.

4. *Find a purpose.*

Forget endless leisure. We don't really want that. Instead, what we want is a sense of purpose to our lives. Each day, we want to feel we're making progress. Psychologists talk about the notion of *flow,* that experience of being totally absorbed in an activity, where you feel competent at what you're doing and where the hours just whiz by. Such moments can give us a profound sense of satisfaction.

Keep this in mind as you think about how you spend your spare time and what you will do in retirement. We imagine we would be happy devoting the rest of our days to lazing around on the couch, watching the tube, playing golf, and reading the newspaper. But we will likely be far happier if we take on challenging tasks that we're likely to succeed at. That might mean training to run a marathon, helping our favorite charity, remodeling the house ourselves, coaching a children's sports team, or going back to college to get a graduate degree.

Indeed, retirement needs to be redefined. If we save diligently, we may be able to cut back the hours we work and we might not need a paycheck at all. But we shouldn't view our nest egg as buying us a life of leisure. Rather, what we're doing is buying ourselves the chance to devote time to those activities we find most rewarding.

5. *Give a little.*

Volunteering isn't just good for the community. It also makes us feel good. In hunter-gatherer societies, where small groups lived in tight communities, it was important to cooperate, to behave well toward others, and to have a good reputation. Maybe it is no great surprise that we enjoy helping our fellow citizens, even if we know we will never see them again.

6. *Make time for friends and family.*

Go out to dinner with the neighbors. Fly across the country to see the grandchildren. Take your spouse to the theater. Host the family reunion. Pay for the family to go to Florida. Or simply invite friends over for a barbeque. Research suggests that spending time with those we love is a huge source of happiness. Looking for a good way to spend your money and your time? Try spending it with friends and family.

## Street Smarts

- As you save diligently for retirement, also give serious thought to how you will fill your days once you quit the workforce—and what will give you a sense of purpose.
- To counteract hedonic adaptation, stop occasionally and contemplate the good things in your life and the good things that have happened.
- As you consider how to spend your time and money, make friends and family a priority.

# Chapter Four

# Even the Best Investors Need to Be Great Savers

*Thrift Doesn't Come Naturally, So Try Trickery*

GIVE ME A CHOICE between some savvy investors and some diligent savers, and I'd bet on the savers every time.

The fact is, committed savers can add so much more to a portfolio's growth. Let's say our savers sock away

20 percent of income each year. That would put them far, far ahead of their fellow Americans, who—as a group—save perilously close to zero. By contrast, if a group of stock mutual fund managers beat the market averages by one or two percentages a year over the course of a decade, the managers would likely be hailed as market-beating heroes. Yet the margin of victory is hardly impressive—and the real heroes would be our diligent savers.

Moreover, for the stock fund managers' success to mean much in terms of dollars and cents, there needs to be a decent sum invested. That, again, is the purview of our committed savers. This isn't a which-came-first-the-chicken-or-the-egg question: Without some initial savings, there is no reward to investing.

## Seeking Inspiration

The need to save, of course, doesn't come as a shocking revelation. Most of us know we ought to be salting away more money. We have all kinds of goals that are desperately important to us, including accumulating enough for the house down payment, funding the kids' college, and paying for our own retirement. But despite all of that, we find it tough to knuckle down and sock away the dollars. Looking for motivation? Here are seven compelling reasons to spend less and save more.

1. The earlier we start saving toward our goals, the easier it will be to amass the necessary money. There are two reasons. First, the required monthly savings will be smaller simply because we can spread the effort over more months. Second, by starting sooner, we will likely get more help from the financial markets, thus further trimming the required monthly savings rate.

2. Spending today doesn't seem to be buying us much happiness. As we learned in the last chapter, the thrill we get from our purchases often fades quickly. Tempted to buy a new car? Before we fork over the necessary dollars or borrow the money involved, maybe we should try a cooling-off period of a week or two. That will give us time to consider whether we will get pleasure commensurate with the money spent.

3. Saving regularly can give us peace of mind. If we know we're living within our means, we are more likely to feel financially content.

4. Saving is a bargain compared to spending. Every dollar we earn and then spend will be subject to federal, state, payroll, and sales taxes, so maybe we end up with 60 or 70 cents' worth of merchandise. Meanwhile, if we stash that dollar in our employer's 401(k) plan, we get to keep the entire dollar

and we can leave it to grow tax-deferred. We may even get a matching company contribution, so our dollar immediately turns into $1.50 or even $2.

5. This brings up a related point: The tax code is stacked in favor of savers. There's a slew of tax-favored accounts, including 401(k) plans, individual retirement accounts, Roth IRAs, Coverdell education savings accounts, and 529 college savings plans. If we are investing through a regular taxable account, we can also take advantage of the low federal tax rate on qualified dividends and long-term capital gains. Moreover, those capital gains taxes don't come due until we sell our winning investments, which means we can postpone the tax bill simply by sitting tight.

6. It doesn't take huge sacrifices to become a top-notch saver. Suppose we step up our savings rate from 5 to 10 percent of our paychecks, thus doubling the amount we save. To achieve this, all that's required is trimming our spending from 95 percent of our paychecks to 90 percent, a drop of just over 5 percent.

7. Diligent savers need smaller retirement nest eggs. If we're big-time savers, we won't just accumulate our desired portfolios more quickly. We will also need less money to retire, because we are accustomed to a lower standard of living.

Indeed, ironically, a big salary increase late in our careers can make it harder to retire. As our salaries climb, we tend to raise our standard of living. That means we now need a larger nest egg to maintain that lifestyle in retirement. The problem is, before we got the pay raise, we were likely saving as though we were looking to replicate a more modest lifestyle. Result: To sustain our new, higher standard of living after we quit the workforce, we either have to save a lot more every month or put off retirement by a few years.

The numbers can be especially daunting once Social Security retirement benefits are figured in. At lower income levels, Social Security can go a long way toward helping retirees maintain their previous standard of living. But at higher income levels, Social Security becomes relatively unimportant—and folks need a heap of savings to replicate their preretirement lifestyle.

## Tying Our Hands

All this raises a key question: If socking away money is critical to investment success and there are so many rational reasons to save, why is there so little of it going on? Once again, we can blame our cave-dwelling ancestors. They weren't interested in delaying gratification. They didn't need self-control. Instead, they immediately consumed whatever they "earned."

Today, we need self-control. But, as most of us can attest, it's a scarce commodity. We tend to eat too much, exercise too little, and spend too freely. To overcome these tendencies, we need to find ways to trick, cajole, and force ourselves to do the right thing.

For instance, to compel ourselves to save, we can sign up for our employer's 401(k) plan, which means the money is deducted from our paycheck before we get a chance to spend it. We might also sign up for automatic mutual fund investment plans, where money is pulled out of our bank accounts every month and invested directly in the funds we choose. This, too, forces us to save. To further bolster our savings, we might commit to rounding up the mortgage check to the nearest $100, so the $1,423 mortgage payment becomes $1,500, thus paying down our loan's principal balance more quickly. We have to pay the mortgage every month anyway, so this is an easy habit to get into. Your mortgage company might even allow you to set up automatic payments that include the additional sum, so that you're locked in to making these extra payments each month.

To save even more, we might create oddball rules for ourselves, such as insisting that we save all tax refunds, year-end bonuses, overtime pay, insurance reimbursements, and money from a second job. Meanwhile, to make sure we don't dip into our savings, we could try "mental accounting," allowing ourselves to spend from our checking accounts, while declaring that our savings, brokerage, mutual fund, and retirement accounts are all off-limits.

We should also be careful to avoid the illusion of saving, socking away a healthy sum each month—but simultaneously piling up the credit card debt. Carrying a credit card balance, and paying the often onerous financing charges, ranks as one of the most foolish financial mistakes.

## Blowing the Budget

In all of this, nowhere have I used the dreaded word *budgeting*. It's an idea that is often lauded by financial experts. Yet, whenever I ask folks whether they budget, the answer is almost always "no"—with good reason. Budgeting doesn't work for most people. When we budget, the idea is to analyze our monthly expenditures, figure out ways to cut back, restrain our spending, and then save whatever remains at the end of the month.

Problem is, we often get to the end of the month and discover there's no money to save. Along the way, we gave into temptation, spent impulsively, blew our budget, and finished the month feeling badly about our spendthrift ways. All in all, budgeting tends to be an unhappy and frustrating experience. We invariably spend more than intended, leaving us racked with remorse.

That's why we are better off forgetting the budget and instead simply socking away money as soon as we get our paycheck. It's the old "pay yourself first" strategy. We immediately salt away 10 or 15 percent of our salary and then force ourselves to live on whatever remains. We know we have taken care of savings. That means we're free to spend our remaining income as we wish, without fussing over some silly budget or fretting that there won't be any money left over to save. Tempted to create a budget? Just say no.

---

### Street Smarts

- If you want your nest egg to grow faster, forget picking superior investments—and instead focus on saving more.
- Force yourself to save by signing up for your employer's 401(k) and arranging to invest automatically in mutual funds.
- Make it a point to sock away tax refunds, year-end bonuses, overtime pay, and any other extra money you receive.

# Chapter Five

# Time Is as Valuable as Money

_Investment Compounding?_
_Yes, It Is Truly Magical_

THE BEST DAY TO START IS TODAY.

Make no mistake: Turning ourselves into committed savers is no easy task. Retirement seems far away. The sums we need to amass appear daunting. Controlling our spending is a struggle.

To make matters worse, our first few years as savers can be awfully discouraging. In those early years, when our nest egg is tiny, we won't get much help from invest-ment gains. Instead, the key driver of our portfolios' growth is the raw dollars we sock away. Yet, if we can get through those discouraging initial years and accumulate a modest portfolio, the rewards can be immense—and we should begin to see the wondrous benefits of starting early.

## Paying Upfront

What benefits? There's the obvious: The earlier we begin saving, the less we need to sock away each month to achieve our goals—and the more help we should get from the finan-cial markets. To get a better handle on the importance of starting young, check out Exhibit 5.1. If you're aiming to amass $1 million by age 65, you would need to sock away a hefty $2,423 a month if you start saving at age 45. But if you begin at age 25, the required monthly sum drops by roughly three quarters, to just $653. These savings rates

**EXHIBIT 5.1   Who Wants to Be a Millionaire?**

*The earlier you start saving, the easier it is to amass your desired sum. Here's how much you need to save each month to accumulate $1 million by age 65, assuming a 5 percent annual return.*

| Starting Age | 25 | 30 | 35 | 40 | 45 | 50 | 55 |
|---|---|---|---|---|---|---|---|
| Required Monthly Savings | $653 | $877 | $1,197 | $1,672 | $2,423 | $3,726 | $6,413 |

assume a steady 5 percent annual return, which might seem low, but we're also assuming zero inflation.

At work here is investment compounding, which is often described as magical, as in the "magic of compounding." And it is truly magical. Suppose you invest $100 and earn 5 percent a year. You would have $105 after one year, $128 after five years, $163 after 10 years, $208 after 15 years, $339 after 25 years, and $1,147 after 50 years. With each passing year, you potentially earn gains not only on your original investment, but also on the gains you scored in earlier years that you reinvested back into your portfolio.

Toss in some regular savings and the numbers become even more impressive. Let's say you save a mere $100 a month and earn 5 percent a year. You would have $1,233 after one year, $6,829 after five years, $15,593 after 10 years, $26,840 after 15 years, $59,799 after 25 years, and $267,977 after 50 years. As the numbers suggest, you won't enjoy much compounding in those early discouraging years, when your nest egg is small. For instance, your portfolio's $6,829 value after five years is just $829 more than your $6,000 cost basis—the actual amount you socked away through your $100 monthly deposit.

But if you persevere, you should reach the point of critical mass, where your annual dollar investment gains begin outstripping the sum you salt away each year. In the

example discussed here, your $100 a month has turned
into $26,840 after 15 years. If that $26,840 earns 5 percent over the next year, you'll garner investment gains of
$1,342, more than the $1,200 you're planning to sock
away. In effect, your nest egg is now firing on all cylinders,
with your savings and your investment gains combining to
power your portfolio's growth.

From that point forward, it should only get better,
with the markets performing the heavy investment lifting.
In many years, your investment gains could dwarf the
amount you're socking away. But all this assumes you
start saving in your first decade or so in the workforce, so
you hit critical mass relatively early in your career. By
contrast, if you put off saving for retirement until your
forties, you won't get nearly so much help from the financial markets—and you'll have to sock away heaps of money
each month to reach your retirement goal.

## Working Late

What if you are late to the retirement savings game—and
the required monthly nut seems too large? You could
turn time to your advantage at the other end of your
career, by postponing retirement for a few years. That
will give you more time to save and more time to collect
investment gains.

You will also shorten your retirement. This means that, when you quit the workforce, you might be able to draw down your nest egg more aggressively and you should get a larger monthly check if you purchase an immediate fixed annuity that pays lifetime income. In addition, if you postpone retirement, you might delay claiming your Social Security retirement benefit and that, too, will mean a larger monthly check.

Hate the idea of staying in the workforce for a few extra years? Consider working part-time instead. On your reduced paycheck, you may not be able to save regularly. But, by working part-time, you could put off the day when you have to tap your nest egg for income. Until then, your portfolio will have time to collect additional investment gains.

## Feeling Virtuous

If you start saving in your twenties and you quickly amass a decent chunk of wealth, you won't just clock years of investment returns. You could also lower your cost of living. After all, if you have some savings, you may be comfortable raising the deductibles on your health, homeowner's, and auto insurance and accepting a longer waiting time before benefits kick in on your disability and long-term care insurance. You may even amass enough savings so that your family would be okay financially if you died—and hence you probably won't need as much life insurance. All of this will lower your insurance costs.

Meanwhile, your growing wealth means you shouldn't ever have to carry a credit card balance and suffer the punishing financing charges that go with it. You may also be able to put down 20 percent when you buy your first home, so you avoid the cost of private mortgage insurance. Similarly, you might pay cash when you buy a car or, at least, hold down the amount you borrow, thus reducing the interest you pay. And when you do borrow, your burgeoning wealth and admirable credit history may mean you qualify for a lower interest rate. Also, you could avoid a slew of irritating fees, including those for bouncing checks, paying bills late, and having financial accounts below some specified minimum. You might even have enough to qualify for the fee reduction on big accounts that are sometimes offered by financial advisers and mutual funds.

Sound appealing? It is. Instead of getting nickeled and dimed in your financial life, you're in control. As you pile up some savings, you can cut your living expenses. That, in turn, will give you even more money to save each month. It's a virtuous cycle—and it could put you on the fast track to financial independence.

## Street Smarts

- To get the most from investment compounding, endeavor to start saving as soon as you enter the workforce.
- If you save regularly for a decade or two, you should reach the point of critical mass, where your annual investment gains often rival the sum you save each year.
- Take advantage of your growing wealth by looking for ways to cut back on insurance, financial account fees, and borrowing costs.

*Chapter Six*

# No Investment Is Risk-Free

~

*It's a Dangerous World—Even
for Those Hiding out in
Savings Accounts*

Now that you're a committed saver, you have to figure out where to stash those monthly savings. Should you go for stocks, with their promise of high returns, or maybe favor certificates of deposit, with their comforting reputation for safety?

Start with this brutal truth: No investment is free of all risk.

Investments can usually be slotted into one of four categories—stocks, bonds, cash investments, and hard assets. How much you invest in each will depend on your goals, your time horizon, and your stomach for risk. This notion of risk, however, can be a tricky one. At times, each of the four may seem like the low-risk option. But don't be lulled into complacency. In the right circumstances, all four can go badly wrong. The good news: All four probably won't go wrong at the same time.

## Sharing the Pain

The four categories of investment are, of course, quite different. Stocks allow you to become part owners of publicly traded corporations, and you should benefit as dividends are paid and rising earnings drive share prices higher. Meanwhile, when you buy bonds and cash investments, you become a lender and earn interest in return for the use of your money. Cash investments like savings accounts and money market funds shouldn't fluctuate in value, while bonds will rise and fall in price as interest rates change. Finally, hard assets encompass a grab bag of investments, including real estate, gold, commodities, and timber, all of which tend to be a good hedge against accelerating inflation.

Folks will look at this menu of choices and make all-or-nothing decisions. "I don't want to lose money, so I'm sticking with money market funds," declare some. "I want the highest possible return, so I'm buying stocks," pronounce others. But these lopsided investment strategies can put you in grave financial peril. You stand to benefit greatly if things go your way, but you also leave yourself heavily exposed to that investment's own peculiar risk.

Stocks, as well as hard assets such as gold shares and commodities, are typically considered the most treacherous of investments, because they can give up 20 percent of their value in a matter of months—and sometimes far, far more. When the stock market slumps, the losses often come with breathtaking speed, as we were reminded in late 2008 and early 2009. To gauge short-term risk, investors often look to statistical measures of volatility, such as standard deviation and beta, which give a sense for how much an investment bounces up and down in price. To be sure, upside volatility—otherwise known as making a truckload of money—may not seem like much of a risk. But upside volatility is frequently a sign of downside potential. In other words, what goes up fast can, unfortunately, come crashing down just as quickly.

You can mute this risk by spreading your money across a host of different stocks. This broad diversification has three benefits. First, it damps down volatility, as the decline in some stocks may be partially or entirely offset by the gains posted by other shares. Second, diversification reduces the risk that you will be wiped out because one or two companies plunge in value. Finally, broad diversification lowers the risk that your returns will lag far behind the market averages. For most people, typically the cheapest and easiest way to get broad diversification is with mutual funds and exchange-traded index funds.

Diversification, however, doesn't eliminate all risk. Even if you own a broad collection of stock funds, the ride is likely to be rough. The good news: In return for suffering the wild short-term price swings, stocks hold out the possibility of healthy long-run returns. This is the classic notion of risk getting rewarded. Stocks are higher risk than bonds, while bonds are higher risk than cash investments. That means a broad collection of shares should beat bonds which, in turn, should beat cash investments. According to academic and other research, stocks have historically been the big winner, beating inflation by seven percentage points a year, while bonds have outpaced inflation by just two or three percentage points, and cash investments have barely beaten inflation at all.

But there are no guarantees stocks will continue to win. After all, if the eventual triumph of stocks was a sure thing, they wouldn't really be risky—and they wouldn't need to offer the prospect of higher returns to get people to buy them. And even if stocks do eventually triumph, you may have to sell before victory is declared. Historically, we have had long periods of lousy stock returns, with share prices going nowhere for a decade or longer. Occasionally, stock investors have been wiped out entirely, as war and political turmoil have caused the closing of some national stock markets. We tend to discount the chance of such extreme events. Yet unfathomable things happen in the financial markets with surprising frequency—and that suggests a little caution is probably in order.

## Hedging Our Bets

The prospect of lousy stock returns and shuttered markets prompts some folks to eschew stocks and load up on bonds and cash investments. Make no mistake: When the financial markets suffer one of their periodic meltdowns, like those of 1987, 1990, 1994, 1998, 2000–2002 and 2008–2009, it's enormously comforting to have a little money in conservative investments. Moreover, if you're retired, prudence dictates keeping some money in bonds, certificates of deposit, and similar conservative investments, so you have a way to get cash without having to sell stocks at fire-sale prices.

Keeping everything in bonds and cash investments, however, has risks of its own. Stocks may suffer rotten short-term results, but they can also deliver healthy long-run returns.

By contrast, bonds and cash investments might offer short-term stability, but they may not provide the returns you need to achieve your financial goals—and they can leave you at the mercy of inflation. In fact, while plunging markets garner the big newspaper headlines, inflation is arguably a far more sinister threat. In the 1970s, it wreaked havoc, running at a brisk 7.4 percent a year, so that during the decade a dollar's spending power shrank to just 49 cents. Even modest inflation can take a toll. Suppose your bonds yield 5 percent and your money market fund kicks off 3 percent. These might seem like reasonable returns—unless inflation is running at 3 percent, at which point your invest-ments are making little or no money.

This is a key reason to own stocks and maybe also keep a portion of your portfolio in hard assets. Historically, stocks have provided long-term protection against infla-tion, thanks to their superior returns. Hard assets may not rival the long-term returns offered by stocks. But they have sometimes provided useful short-term protection, posting gains when accelerating inflation has caused stocks and bonds to slump. For further inflation protec-tion, you might allocate a significant portion of your bond portfolio to inflation-indexed Treasury bonds. The principal value of these bonds and the interest they gener-ate rise along with inflation.

All this leaves many investors in a quandary. They don't like the modest returns from high quality bonds and cash investments, but they also don't like the volatility of stocks and hard assets. What to do? For many, the best solution is to own a little of everything, buying bonds and cash investments for downside protection, purchasing hard assets as a defense against unexpected inflation, and investing in stocks for their long-run returns. That strategy will never earn you the highest possible performance, but it will limit your portfolio's risk. And risk is well worth focusing on. You can't be sure how the various markets will perform—but you can control how much risk you take.

## Compromising Our Future

Seem reasonable? Some don't think so and they go searching for alternatives. The result is often an unhappy compromise. For instance, some investors stick with income-paying investments, like bonds and preferred stock, but they hunt for securities that promise hefty payouts. The problem is, there can be a big difference between yield and total return. An investment's total return takes into account not only the yield that gets paid, but also any changes in the investment's price. The danger: You get the fat yield, at least for a while, but you end up putting your principal at risk. Consider high-yield junk bond funds. These funds often boast double-digit yields. But part of that gain may slip away, as some junk bond issuers go bust and the defaults drag down the share price of those funds that own these bonds.

Other folks favor investments or strategies that seem to offer both upside potential and downside protection in a single package. Writing covered call options, market-timing mutual funds and equity-indexed annuities all aim to combine these twin goals. But they may end up giving you the worst of both worlds, delivering mediocre returns and involving hefty costs.

Yet others flock to investments that hold out the prospect of high returns but appear to offer safety. That appearance stems from the absence of daily pricing. Think about investments like real estate, hedge funds, private companies, and private loans. These can feel safe because we don't see the daily turmoil that can afflict stocks, bonds, and other readily traded securities. But the fact is, if these investments offer high returns, they must involve high risk. We may not see the price drop day by day, but we can wake up one morning and discover we have lost a big chunk of our investment.

My advice: Be leery of these alternatives, stick with the simplicity of plain-vanilla, low cost mutual funds—and work instead on your expectations. For instance, you might mentally divide your nest egg into *safe money* and *growth money,* and then tailor your expectations accordingly. Invest the growth money in stock funds and riskier bond funds, expect a wild ride, and hope to get rewarded for it. Meanwhile, stash your safe money in conservative investments, knowing the returns won't be great but also knowing you will get stability. When the markets are flying high, enjoy your growth money's gains. When markets plunge, turn to your safe money for solace. But that still leaves a crucial question: How should you divvy up your nest egg between safe money and growth money?

That is where we turn next.

## Street Smarts

- The four big investment categories—stocks, bonds, hard assets, and cash investments—all have their risks, so avoid betting everything on any one of these categories.
- As you design your portfolio, focus not only on reducing the chance of devastating short-term losses, but also on fending off the long-run threat from inflation.
- Mentally divide your portfolio into growth money and safe money—and expect a rough ride from the former and comfort from the latter.

## Chapter Seven

# Portfolio Performance: It's All in the Mix

*Our Stock-Bond Split Powers
Our Investment Results*

THE DECISIONS DON'T GET MUCH BIGGER THAN THIS.

How should you split your money between stocks and more conservative investments, such as high quality bonds, certificates of deposit, and money market funds? As the last chapter suggested, this basic mix will heavily influence how erratically your portfolio performs in the short term.

But it should also drive your long-run return. Want to boost your nest egg's performance? Forget trying to pick high-flying stocks and winning mutual funds. The road to success may be far, far easier.

## Bolstering Returns

Let's start with the obvious. We can't expect stock-like returns from high quality bonds, certificates of deposits, and other conservative investments. And, unless things go badly wrong, we shouldn't get bond-like returns from our stocks over the long haul. Indeed, the basic asset-allocation decision—how we divide our money between stocks, bonds, cash investments, and hard assets—is one of the most crucial financial choices we make. This key decision not only drives our portfolios' short-term fluctuations, but also it will have a huge impact on our long-run performance. The implication: If we want to improve our returns, we might simply allocate more of our money to stocks.

Suppose you have 60 percent of your money in stocks and 40 percent in bonds, and you expect stocks to clock 10 percent a year and bonds to notch 5 percent. With a 60 percent stock–40 percent bond mix, you're looking at an 8 percent expected portfolio return—though, of course, there is no guarantee your expectations will be met. To increase returns, you could bump up your stock allocation to 70 percent. That would raise your portfolio's expected return to 8.5 percent without doing anything particularly clever, like picking better stocks, selecting superior mutual funds, or trying to guess which way the stock market is headed. It is one of the easiest ways to bolster your potential return, and yet one rarely discussed.

Before you go ahead and boost your stock holdings, consider three caveats. I alluded to two of them in the last chapter. First, there's no assurance stocks will outperform more conservative investments. Theory says they should. After all, why would people take the risk of owning stocks if they couldn't reasonably expect a higher reward? That reward, however, is not guaranteed. If it were, there wouldn't be any risk involved.

Second, even if the broad stock market fares just fine, there is a chance your portfolio will perform far worse and thus allocating more to stocks won't help your overall investment performance. One popular Wall Street rule of thumb says you need just 12 to 20 stocks to be well diversified. And with 20 stocks, you could indeed diversify away a lot of the individual business risk associated with any one stock. The trouble is, you might still earn returns that are radically different from the market averages. This is the problem of tracking error—and to combat it you really need to own hundreds of different stocks. To get this sort of broad market exposure, consider purchasing mutual funds and exchange-traded index funds, which can give you a stake in a wide array of companies for a relatively modest investment.

That brings us to a third warning: Nobody should be all stocks. If you're 100 percent in stocks, you can noticeably reduce risk, with very little impact on returns, by adding a small position in bonds. That small stake in bonds will also provide psychological comfort and a little buying power when stocks suffer one of their periodic drubbings. It's tough to sit tight during bear markets. What to do? If you own bonds, you could do something constructive, like take advantage of the market decline by shifting some of your bond market money into stocks.

## Feeling Queasy

Even if the idea of allocating more to stocks sounds appealing, you need to weigh how much risk you can reasonably take—and how much you can truly stomach. The first part is fairly easy and it's based heavily on time horizon. Those approaching retirement, and who will soon be living off their savings, should go lighter on stocks and stock funds. Meanwhile, those far from retirement, and who have a regular paycheck to cover ongoing expenses, can take the risk of investing more heavily in the stock market.

As you consider this general guidance, keep two things in mind. First, as noted in Chapter One, you may want to invest more conservatively if your job isn't particularly secure or your paycheck fluctuates widely. Second, you won't spend your entire nest egg on the day you retire, so you don't need to be completely out of stocks when you quit the workforce. In fact, faced with a retirement that could last 25 or 30 years, you might keep half your money in stock funds.

With other goals, the deadlines are more cut-and-dried. You will need the money for the house down payment on a particular day. You will spend your child's college savings over four years. With these deadlines in mind, you should probably look to ease out of stocks when you are five years from spending the money involved. Over some five-year stretches, stocks have lost money. By contrast, if you have 10 years to invest, history indicates you should at least break even with stocks and you will likely make good money.

Given all that, you probably shouldn't invest in the stock market unless you have a minimum of seven or eight years to invest—and, once you're within five years of needing your money, you should start looking to sell. That doesn't mean you should unload your stocks when you are five years out, regardless of market conditions. If stocks are in the middle of a brutal bear market, you might sit tight for a little longer and hope prices bounce back. But if stocks are buoyant and you're five years from needing the money, you should probably take the chance to shift out of stocks and into conservative investments.

While a quick consideration of time horizon can help you figure out how much risk you can reasonably take, it is far tougher to gauge how much risk you can stomach. Everybody's risk tolerance is different, and the portfolio you're comfortable with may be radically different from that favored by somebody of the same age with the same goals and the same time horizon.

Moreover, our risk tolerance isn't stable. It's easy to be big and brave during rip-roaring bull markets. It is a lot harder during those relentless bear market declines, when the pundits are full of doom and gloom and your neighbors are panicking and selling. Want to know how you'll react to the next market downturn? Forget the risk-tolerance questionnaires—and instead recall your behavior during previous bear markets. In fact, you probably shouldn't invest a high percentage of your money in stocks until you've lived through a 20 percent-plus stock market decline. During that decline, think about how much you are comfortable investing in stocks—and then use that as your guideline thereafter.

## Hitting the Target

Once you have decided what percentage of your money you will allocate to stocks, you need to stick close to that target. Let's say you opt for 70 percent stocks. Bull markets will increase the value of your stocks and stock funds, pushing your percentage above 70 percent. To get your portfolio back on target, you will want to rebalance occasionally, selling some of your stocks and moving the proceeds to bonds and other parts of your portfolio that have become underweighted. Similarly, during bear markets, your stock allocation will fall below 70 percent and you will want to do some buying, to get your stock allocation back up to 70 percent.

If, during bear markets, you rebalance back into stocks, it will help your portfolio recover more quickly when the markets bounce back. But in general, rebalancing between stocks and more conservative investments will hurt your long-run returns. Most of the time, you will likely be cutting back on stocks, which should be your best-performing asset. Indeed, if you wanted higher returns, you would avoid rebalancing.

So why rebalance? It's about controlling risk. By rebalancing back to your target stock percentage, you keep your portfolio in line with the risk level you originally settled on. If you didn't rebalance, your portfolio would grow increasingly risky as your stocks rise in value—and that means you could get hit especially hard during the next bear market.

Rebalancing is best done within a retirement account. That way, you don't trigger an immediate tax bill if you sell stocks with big capital gains. If you need to rebalance within a taxable account, first see if you can get your portfolio back into line with your target percentages by directing new savings and any dividends, interest, and mutual fund distributions to those areas of your portfolio that have become underweighted.

While rebalancing is about risk control, it has the added virtue of giving you something to do. Earlier, I mentioned that keeping a little money in bonds will give you some buying power, which you can put to good use when share prices tumble. Similarly, rebalancing also offers a plan of attack, one that can ease a lot of bear market anxiety. At times of financial turmoil, when investors are gripped by a sense of crisis and many are frozen by fear, it can be enormously comforting to have a well-defined investment strategy—and the chance to put it into action.

---

### Street Smarts

- When deciding what portion of your portfolio to stash in stocks, consider how much risk you can reasonably take—and how much you can truly stomach.
- As you approach retirement, you may want to lighten up on stocks. But you probably shouldn't abandon the stock market entirely.
- Every year or so, look to rebalance by bringing your stocks, bonds, hard assets, and cash investments back into line with your target percentages.

# Chapter Eight

# Stocks Are Worth *Something*

⁓

## Getting a Piece of the Economic Action

MANY FOLKS VIEW BUYING STOCKS as little better than gambling, and it's easy to understand why.

Stocks soar one day and sink the next, while billions of shares change hands and pundits wring their hands over the market's direction. Meanwhile, investors vacillate between delight and despair, last year's whiz-kid money manager becomes this year's whipping boy and the current hot stock turns into next year's bankruptcy filing. All in all, the market seems like one big crapshoot—and it's hardly surprising people shy away from stocks and stock funds, especially at times of market turmoil.

Yet there's more to stocks than ticker symbols, stock certificates, and ever-changing share prices. Stocks represent partial ownership in publicly traded corporations, offering a chance to share in global business prosperity. Expect world economies to continue growing? With any luck, stocks will go along for the ride.

## Keeping Grounded

Indeed, as we're whipsawed by yo-yoing share prices, it's important to keep economic fundamentals in mind, so we stick with our stocks and have a shot at earning those impressive long-run gains. Over the 50 years through year-end 2007, gross domestic product climbed at an average 7 percent a year, according to the U.S. Department of Commerce's Bureau of Economic Analysis. That economic growth drove up corporate profits by 7 percent a year, which, in turn, propelled stocks to a 7 percent annual price gain. Tack on dividends, and you push the stock market's average annual total return well above 10 percent.

To be sure, this simplistic description calls for all kinds of caveats. Share prices didn't rise in lockstep with economic growth. In many years, stocks didn't come close to delivering 10 percent—and we might not average 10 percent a year in the future. In addition, the full benefits of economic growth may not flow through to shareholders if management reinvests profits incompetently or issues huge numbers of new shares.

Still, during stock market bloodbaths like 2000 to 2002 and 2008 to 2009, it is helpful to take a deep breath and consider the three components of the stock market's return. First, there is corporate earnings growth. Yes, that growth will suffer during recessions. But unless we get an economic apocalypse, we should see moderate earnings growth over the long haul, as the expanding economy pushes up corporate profits.

Second, there are the dividends that corporations pay using a portion of those earnings. In a recession, some companies will cut or eliminate their dividends. But if you own a diversified portfolio of stocks, the impact shouldn't be too severe. The implication: If you buy a collection of stocks that yield, say, 3 percent, you can reasonably expect to collect that 3 percent.

But while earnings should climb over time and dividends are fairly reliable, the third component of the market's return is far less certain. We're talking here about the value put on corporate profits, as reflected in the stock market's price-earnings multiple. An example: If a company's stock is at $30 and it had earnings per share of $2 over the past year, its stock would be trading at 15 times earnings. Price-earnings multiples soar and sink, as investors flit between giddy exuberance and nail-biting despair. In the early 1980s, stocks traded below seven times earnings, while in the late 1990s we got above 30 times earnings. That's an enormous swing in valuation. In fact, in the short term, changes in the market's price-earnings ratio will often have by far the largest impact on stock returns, easily swamping the benefit of earnings growth and dividends paid.

## Looking Downfield

Over the long term, however, it's a different story. The influence of price-earnings ratios starts to wane—and earnings growth and dividends become the key drivers of stock performance. Imagine you are investing for a retirement that's 35 years away. Over that stretch, the market's price-earnings multiple contracts from 20 to 10, earnings climb 7 percent a year and dividends are 3 percent. The combination of earnings growth and dividends would ordinarily give you a 10 percent total return. But the halving of the market's P/E ratio clearly hurts results. Yet, over 35 years, the impact isn't all that great and you would still collect an average 8 percent a year.

Moreover, if you invested regularly over those 35 years, you could take advantage of the market's contracting P/E by purchasing shares at lower valuations. Admittedly, it takes a strong stomach to buy when stock prices are tumbling. But that's why it is important to keep in mind that stocks aren't mere pieces of paper. As the market falls, its expected long-term return rises. Shares are now cheaper relative to dividends and corporate profits, which suggests better performance thereafter.

Indeed, while tumbling share prices typically cause investors to turn cautious, the rational response is to become more optimistic. To understand why, forget stocks for a moment—and consider the example of bonds. Bond prices and yields move in opposite directions, so that yields rise as bond prices fall. Because the bulk of your bond return comes from the yield, the benefits of falling prices are all too clear. Yields are now higher, so returns thereafter should be better—a notion that even the most naïve investors tend to grasp. Even if you have no additional money to invest in bonds, you can take advantage of the new, higher yield by reinvesting your interest payments. Result: Rising interest rates can hurt your bond portfolio's value in the short term, while simultaneously raising its expected long-run return.

Similarly, falling share prices should make you more enthused about stocks and you can take advantage of the decline by reinvesting your dividends. But given that stock dividend yields are usually lower than bond yields, reinvesting your dividends won't give you much buying power. Instead, if you really want to profit from slumping share prices, you need to step up the amount you invest each month and also consider rebalancing. If you keep fundamentals in mind, maybe you'll have the courage to do just that.

What if stocks rise? Rather than becoming more enthusiastic about purchasing stocks, you should become less so. But that doesn't mean you should stop saving money every month. True, if we have great returns over the past year, you may now be closer than expected to amassing your target nest egg. But remember, if stocks have raced ahead of the underlying growth in corporate earnings, the past year's big market gain may have effectively borrowed from the future—and weaker returns may lie ahead. As a result, you may not want to buy more stocks, because they are now more richly valued. But because there is a risk future returns will be lower, it's prudent to keep saving. What to do? Instead of purchasing more stocks, you might use your monthly savings to buy bonds.

## Street Smarts

- Whenever stocks soar or sink, temper your enthusiasm or fear by keeping economic fundamentals in mind.
- Take advantage of falling share prices by rebalancing, reinvesting dividends, and increasing your monthly purchases.
- If stocks skyrocket, continue saving—but consider buying bonds instead.

# Chapter Nine

# To Add Wealth, We Need to Overcome the Subtractions

—— ❧ ——

*If We Aren't Careful, We'll Double Our Money—in 47 Years*

GETTING IT IS ONE THING. Keeping it is another.

The financial markets can post astonishing one-year returns, such as the 30 percent-plus gains clocked by the Dow Jones Wilshire 5000 stock index in 1985, 1991, 1995, 1997, and 2003. Indeed, at times, Wall Street can seem like a magic money machine, minting millionaires on a daily basis.

But dig a little deeper and you find investors aren't faring nearly as well as the raw returns suggest. Why not? At issue here is the triple threat of investment costs, taxes, and inflation. If your portfolio isn't overcoming those big three subtractions, you aren't making any money.

## Slipping Away

Imagine you hold a classic balanced portfolio, consisting of 60 percent stocks and 40 percent bonds. Before all subtractions, that mix delivers 8 percent a year, which is enough to double your money every nine years, thanks to investment compounding. But even if your investments earn an 8 percent raw return, you will pocket far less if you're careless about investment costs and taxes. For instance, you could easily lose two percentage points a year and possibly more to mutual fund expenses and other costs. That would turn your 8 percent return into 6 percent. If you're sloppy about taxes and you are in the 25 percent federal income tax bracket, that 6 percent may become 4.5 percent. Inflation might then steal another three percentage points, leaving you with just 1.5 percent a year. At that rate, it would take 47 years to double your money.

Sound grim? You can't do anything about the inflation rate. You also can't insist on better market performance.

But there's much you *can* do. For starters, you can be sensible about risk, avoiding big bets on one or two stocks or on a single market sector. You can also remain disciplined in the face of market turbulence, restraining your greed during bull markets and resisting panicky decisions when share prices decline.

Maybe more important, in reference to our current example, you can pick low-expense investments—or ask your adviser to pick them for you—and you can strive to invest in a tax-efficient manner. Take our 8 percent pre-cost, pre-tax, pre-inflation return. Without too much effort, you could probably cut your investment costs in half, to one percentage point or so every year, leaving you with a 7 percent after-cost return. If you then bought your investments inside a retirement account, you would get tax-deferred and possibly tax-free growth, so you hang on to the full 7 percent. You can read more about the benefits of retirement accounts in Chapters Seventeen and Eighteen. To be sure, you would still suffer the full fury of inflation, which is knocking three percentage points off your return. Nonetheless, instead of notching 1.5 percent a year after inflation, you would be making closer to 4 percent, enough to double your money every 18 years. See Exhibit 9.1.

The difference between 1.5 percent and 4 percent might not seem like much. But over time, the gap would be enormous, thanks to compounding. If you save $100 a

**EXHIBIT 9.1   Cheap Thrills**

*By favoring lower-cost investments and using tax-favored retirement accounts, you could greatly improve your results. The example here assumes an investor is in the 25 percent tax bracket.*

|  | Higher-Cost Strategy | Lower-Cost Strategy |
| --- | --- | --- |
| Annual return | 8% | 8% |
| Minus costs | 2 | 1 |
| Minus taxes | 1.5 | 0 |
| Minus inflation | 3 | 3 |
| Real return | 1.5% | 4% |

month and earn 4 percent a year, you would have $118,600 after four decades. If you earn just 1.5 percent, you would pocket a mere $65,800.

## Trimming the Tab

Sound simple enough? It is—and yet many people pay precious little attention to investment costs and taxes. This partly reflects investors' single-minded focus on performance. They are so anxious to find the next hot stock or the next superstar mutual fund that they fail to notice how much they're losing to costs and taxes. But this partly also reflects the way investment costs and taxes are paid. We file our tax returns long after we make our trades and long after we collect our dividends, interest, and mutual fund distributions. Not surprisingly, the connection between the investment decisions we made and the taxes we pay seems tenuous, at best.

Meanwhile, whether we invest on our own or we use a financial adviser, it is rare that we receive a separate bill for the investment costs we incur, so it's hard to track how much we're paying. Account maintenance fees and asset management fees are often subtracted directly from our portfolios. Mutual fund expenses are gradually deducted throughout the year. Commissions are usually rolled into an investment's purchase price or subtracted out of the sales proceeds. The other big trading cost is the *bid-ask spread,* which is the difference between the higher price at which market makers will sell us a stock and the lower price at which they will buy it back. This spread can go entirely unnoticed, because it's built into the price. But sometimes, this spread will cost us more than the brokerage commission charged on the trade.

True, we can't avoid all investment costs. If we buy mutual funds or hire financial advisers, we should fully expect to pay for their services. Instead, the goal is to understand what we are paying—and to ensure the bill isn't so onerous that we're unlikely to earn decent returns.

Take mutual fund expenses. Many bond mutual funds charge almost 1 percent a year, equal to $1 for every $100 we have invested, while stock funds often charge around 1.5 percent, equal to $1.50 for every $100 invested. Such costs might seem inconsequential if we manage to invest with some hotshot fund manager. But as you will learn in the next chapter, picking winners isn't easy. Most fund managers don't perform well enough to recoup the fees they charge, which means the typical mutual fund lags behind its benchmark index.

Indeed, differences in annual fund expenses are a key driver of differences in fund performance. This is especially clear with bond and money market funds. Over a five-year stretch, each bond and money fund category's top performers are almost always the funds with the lowest annual expenses. Costs aren't quite as big a determinant of differences in stock fund performance. A stock fund manager can get lucky and post big gains despite the burden of a hefty expense ratio. Still, it makes sense to stack the odds in your favor by sticking with lower-cost funds.

If you use a financial adviser, you can get your adviser to do the cost-cutting for you. Today, you might pay around 1 percent a year for a financial adviser's help. If you don't have much money to invest, you may pay somewhat more. If you have a seven-figure portfolio, you might pay less. This 1 percent or so can be charged in a variety of ways. Some advisers get compensated through commissions, some charge a percentage of a portfolio's value, some bill by the hour, and some levy a monthly or annual retainer. If you pay a retainer or a percentage of assets, the sum you're charged will be fairly steady from year to year. If you pay commissions or by the hour, the amount could vary sharply.

In return for this fee, your adviser might provide all manner of financial assistance, including building you a sensible portfolio, encouraging you to save, counseling calm at times of market turmoil, and helping with other aspects of your financial life. To your adviser's list of duties, consider adding one other item: cutting your investment costs. Today, depending on the type of portfolio your adviser is looking to build, she could get your fund expenses down to 0.2 percent a year or even less. In fact, by slashing your investment expenses, your adviser could go a long way toward justifying her fee.

But where can you find funds with such low costs? It's time for Chapter Ten.

## Street Smarts

- Fret less about short-term performance and focus more on items you have some control over, like how much risk you take, your trading costs, and your investment tax bill.
- Figure out how much you're paying in investment costs—and make sure the tab isn't so onerous that you're unlikely to earn decent returns.
- If you use an adviser, task the adviser with trimming your fund expenses and other costs.

Chapter Ten

# Aiming for Average Is the Only Sure Way to Win

*Why the Meek Will Inherit the Earth*

TO EARN HEALTHY RETURNS, we need to take risk. But what if our risk-taking isn't rewarded?

This, I fear, is an all-too-common occurrence. Hungry for supercharged returns, investors bet heavily on a few stocks or some high-flying stock mutual funds, only to find that they're earning lackluster returns as the broad market charges ahead. But such setbacks don't deter the gambling set. These folks roll the dice again and again, hoping that their luck will turn. Like lottery ticket buyers, they are buoyed by the occasional small win and they dream of the investment jackpot. But the jackpot never gets hit and their eventual retirement proves to be a penny-pinching affair.

Their mistake: These folks fundamentally misunderstand what stock market investing is all about. We don't invest to beat the market, get rich, or earn the highest possible return. Money isn't an end in itself. Rather, it is a means to other ends. We invest to meet our goals, whether it's buying a home, putting the kids through college, or paying for our own retirement.

## Meeting Our Match

What strategy will give us the greatest chance of reaching our goals? Earning market-beating investment returns would certainly help. Trouble is, if we try to beat the stock market, we also run the risk of lagging behind. The two outcomes, however, are far from equal. In one scenario, we retire richer. In the other, we may not retire at all. Given that we all get just a single shot at saving and investing for retirement, it makes sense to avoid strategies that could put our retirement at risk, such as betting the bank on a single stock or a single market sector.

Nonetheless, we remain fixated on beating the market. We see stocks that climb 100 or 200 percent in a single year. We read about superstar mutual funds. We hear about hot little companies with nifty new inventions. We watch great corporations grow steadily year after year. We see how, with apparent predictability, winners turn into losers and bull markets turn into bear markets. The easy money, it appears, is there for the taking. It seems so simple to pick winning stocks, find superstar funds, and sidestep market declines.

And yet it isn't. Outpacing the market over an extended period is so difficult that the rare winners—such as Warren Buffett, chairman of Berkshire Hathaway—are hailed for their investment acumen and treated like celebrities.

Why do so few triumph? Here are 10 reasons.

1. *Costs drag down results.*

    As discussed in Chapter Nine, investment costs can put a big dent in our returns. The logic, I am afraid, is brutally simple. Before investment costs, we collectively earn the stock market averages. After costs, we must—as a group—lag behind. In fact, we will collectively trail the market by an amount equal to our costs. Some lucky souls will overcome this harsh arithmetic and emerge victorious, but most of us won't.

This logic is especially troubling for those hell-bent on beating the market. We like to think that hard work will pay off when investing, just as it pays dividends in other parts of our lives. The problem is, working hard at investing often means incurring more investment costs, whether it's research expenses, money management fees, or trading costs. And therein lies the rub. The more we spend trying to beat the market, the tougher it is to succeed.

2. *Markets are smart.*

Even if most investors fail, maybe you could find a way to win. One obstacle: Markets are reasonably efficient, meaning they reflect currently available information. Take XYZ Corporation. Analysts, on average, expect its earnings to climb an impressive 30 percent over the next year. But that's hardly a reason to buy the stock. Investors already know about those expectations, so they are presumably fairly fully reflected in the company's share price.

Instead, what drives markets is news, which—by definition—is something we hadn't previously known about. That news might be a change in an analyst's earnings forecast, the latest economic data, a corporate earnings announcement, some political development, or even an offhand comment by a company executive. Once this news breaks, it is quickly built into stock prices, so it's tough to profit even if we react immediately.

All this can be discouraging if you're aiming to outpace the market. Because markets quickly incorporate all known information, it is hard to get an edge, no matter how well informed you are. But what hurts the savvy helps the ignorant. Uninformed investors are protected by market efficiency. They may shoot themselves in the foot by trading too much and making risky bets. Still, when they buy a stock, they can be reasonably confident that the share price reflects all currently available information.

3. *The competition is tough.*

You are unlikely to dig up information that others don't already have and that isn't already built into market prices. You could, however, do a better job of analyzing existing information. But will you? As you confidently buy and sell, you may imagine yourself competing against *the market,* some bloated entity that you can easily outwit. But in truth, you are competing against other investors. Consider again XYZ Corporation, with its expected 30 percent profit growth. You have analyzed the company's financial statements, you've considered the firm's market position, and you believe corporate profits will be even better than analysts expect.

As you load up on the shares, there will be investors on the other side of the trade, happily dumping their stock. They, too, have no doubt analyzed the company's financials, considered its market position, and wondered about its growth potential. And they may be professional money managers with business degrees, high-powered computers, years of experience, and access to the latest stock market research. Are you sure you know more than they do?

I am not trying to dissuade you from ever again buying or selling an investment. If you're going to retire in comfort, you will need to pick out a diverse collection of mutual funds that give you broad market exposure, add to them regularly, and occasionally revamp the mix. Nonetheless, as you manage your portfolio, a little humility is in order. Maybe the folks on the other side of the trade really do know something you don't—so maybe you shouldn't bet too heavily on any one stock or stock market sector.

4. *No strategy always wins.*

There are all kinds of strategies for selecting individual stocks. Some investors look for high-flying growth stocks, or growth at a reasonable price, or high-dividend stocks, or stocks that are trading below their intrinsic value. For a while, any one of these strategies might be highly profitable.

But don't count on them being always profitable. Partly, that's because of the costs involved in implementing these and any other investment strategy. But partly, too, it reflects the competitiveness of the market. If a stock-picking strategy proves superior, it quickly becomes popular. Soon, legions of investors are using the same criteria to pick stocks and their buying drives up the price of the favored companies. Because prices are higher, future returns will be lower—and the strategy stops working.

5. *Investment trends die.*

Okay, maybe you'll forget the dicey business of picking individual stocks. Instead, you will look to ride the hottest market sectors, betting on them by buying a basket of stocks or a narrowly focused mutual fund. That way, it doesn't matter if a few stocks crash and burn.

At first blush, this doesn't seem so foolish. There's some evidence of momentum in the stock market. Investments that perform well one year often continue to fare well in the year that follows. It may be that, when prospects improve for a company or a sector, investors initially under-react to the good news. But as the good news continues to flow,

doubtful investors become believers and these investments extend their winning streak. Because of this
sort of market momentum, if you own an investment
that posts strong short-term results, you probably
shouldn't be too quick to cash in your gains.

But that doesn't mean you should rush to buy in
to hot sectors. It's hard to make money from market momentum, especially if you're doing a heap of
trading and thus incurring high investment costs.
Moreover, timing these things is tricky. Some market trends never gain traction. Some last far longer
than expected. Those who bail out early are left
kicking themselves. Those who buy late may see
the trend as invincible and further gains as inevitable. But such trends always come to an end, sometimes with a whimper, and sometimes with a bang.
Think about health care stocks in the early 1990s,
technology shares in the late 1990s, and housing
stocks during the recent real estate boom. At their
dizzying peak, buyers were convinced these sectors
would generate dazzling gains for years to come and
prices raced far ahead of what economic fundamentals would justify. But the fundamentals eventually
prevailed and these sectors plunged back to earth.

One additional warning: Some investors imagine that if they buy, say, an aggressive growth stock

fund, the manager might be able to sidestep the carnage if the sector goes into a tailspin. This, I regret, is unlikely. Most managers aren't that prescient. But even if they were, funds tend to have tight investment charters that restrict their managers to picking securities from one part of the market. If that part of the market suffers, so will the fund's shareholders.

6. *Gains come quickly.*

Glance at any long-term stock market chart, with its prolonged climbs and punishing bear markets, and the appeal of market timing becomes obvious. If you could sell before the declines and buy before the rebounds, you could make out like a bandit.

This, unfortunately, is easier said than done. There's no surefire indicator that tells you when stocks are about to plunge or soar. Wait too long to buy or sell and you could easily miss your chance, because market gains and losses often come in quick bursts. Market timing can also mean hefty trading costs and, if attempted outside of a retirement account, big tax bills as well.

7. *Nothing recedes like success.*

That brings us to another possibility. Instead of picking your own stocks, maybe you could turn over responsibility to some celebrated stock fund managers and rely on them to make the right investment calls. Even if these managers can't side-step market declines, maybe they could beat the market by a few percentage points each year by picking superior stocks.

Alas, the history of actively managed stock funds is a sorry one. On average, stock-fund managers lag behind their benchmark indexes. You, of course, have no intention of buying average managers. Instead, you plan to buy managers with superior records. But many apparently superior managers quickly revert to average. They may have had a good run simply because their stock-picking style or the sectors they favor were briefly popular.

Other managers continue to thrive. But even if they are truly skillful, their success may contain the seeds of its own destruction. Successful mutual funds grow so popular and so big that their superior returns are hard to sustain. The managers of these funds may also grow overconfident, trading too much and taking on too much risk. That means shareholders of actively managed funds need to remain vigilant, prepared to move on if a fund's glory days appear to be over.

8. *Skill may turn out to be luck.*

To make matters worse, it's difficult for most of us to separate savvy managers from the merely lucky. In fact, success seems so arbitrary that money managers have been compared to monkeys throwing darts at the newspaper stock tables or gamblers flipping coins.

Fair comparisons? Suppose that, as with getting heads with a coin flip, there is a 50 percent chance of beating the market each year (which, given costs, overstates the odds of success). Start with a million investors and, by the end of a dozen years, probability suggests you would have 244 investors who had beaten the market every year. These 244 would, no doubt, be celebrated as market-beating geniuses and crowned the next Warren Buffetts. But are these folks really skillful— or just lucky coin flippers who came up heads 12 times in a row?

The bottom line: Simply identifying funds with good 5- or 10-year records isn't enough. To analyze money manager performance properly and separate the skillful from the lucky takes top-notch information, careful analysis, and keen insight. And even if you have all of that—and most ordinary investors don't—nothing is guaranteed.

9. *The deck is stacked.*

All this may have you scratching your head. After all, most years, there are those spectacular winners, the stocks that double or triple in value. These big winners make beating the market seem easy. Yet, ironically, their very existence means you're more likely to lose. To understand why, imagine a market with 10 stocks. One gains 100 percent this year, while the other nine climb 10 percent. The average gain is 19 percent, but only one stock beat this average and the rest earned far less.

In a less extreme form, this sort of *skewness* often occurs in the stock market. Each year, the market's best stocks might leap 150 percent, 200 percent, or more, while the worst performers can't lose more than 100 percent of their value. The big winners can skew the market average upward far more than the losers can drag it down—which is why a majority of stocks often end up with below-average performance. The big winners may tempt you to bet heavily on a handful of companies. But if you do that, the odds suggest you won't pick superstar stocks and you will suffer lackluster performance. Instead, if you want a good shot at keeping up with the market averages, you should diversify as broadly as possible, thus increasing the odds that you will own some of the big winners.

10. *Investing is counterintuitive.*

If the preceding nine points tell you anything, they should tell you how utterly maddening investing is. Big winners mean you're more likely to lose. Popularity leads to failure. Success contains the seeds of its own destruction. Past performance doesn't repeat. Information isn't necessarily helpful. And hard work can backfire. Maybe it's no great surprise that most of us struggle when investing—so maybe it's no great surprise that there are so few Warren Buffetts.

## Matching the Market

All this can be a tad depressing. Feel like giving up? Great idea. Enter indexing, my favorite investment strategy—a strategy you can use whether you're a do-it-yourself investor or you employ a financial adviser.

Think about the dilemma we face. We get only one shot at investing for retirement, and the cost of failure is far greater than the benefits of success. We also know that trying to succeed, by endeavoring to beat the market, is highly likely to fail. What we need is a strategy that has a greater probability of success.

And that's what indexing offers. An index fund doesn't try to beat the market. Instead, it meekly buys many or all of the securities that make up an index in an effort to replicate the index's performance. That index might be a stock market index, like the Standard & Poor's 500 or the Dow Jones Wilshire 5000, or it might be a bond index, such as the Barclays Capital U.S. Aggregate Bond Index. An index fund will almost always fall somewhat short of its benchmark index because—unlike the underlying index—the fund charges expenses. Still, those expenses might be just 0.2 percent a year, so the shortfall should be modest. Index funds also tend to trade sparingly, which means they're slow to realize their taxable gains and they don't incur a lot of trading costs. Meanwhile, most active investors, with their higher expenses, will trail the market by far more. Result: By aiming for average, the humble index fund ends up winning.

That doesn't mean index funds guarantee you will make money. If the underlying index suffers terrible performance, the funds that track the index will also suffer terribly. But unlike investors who try to beat the market, index fund investors enjoy what's called relative certainty. Their fortunes may rise and fall with the underlying index. But they can be confident that they will capture the index's performance, minus their investment costs. Active investors, who are endeavoring to beat the market, can have no such confidence.

You can now purchase index funds that track all manner of indexes. For instance, to build a globally diversified portfolio, you might buy three index funds, one that replicates the broad U.S. stock market, one that mimics foreign stock markets and one that tracks high quality U.S. bonds. You could get fancier still, adding index funds that replicate the performance of emerging markets stocks, commodities, real estate investment trusts, and other niche markets. You could also buy specialized funds that favor growth stocks, with their potential for rapid earnings and revenue increases, or value stocks, which appear cheap compared to current earnings or corporate assets. Broad-based U.S. funds tend to have the lowest expenses, while more specialized funds and those focused on foreign markets typically charge somewhat more.

Index funds are available as both mutual funds and exchange-traded index funds. With a mutual fund, you can purchase shares directly from the mutual fund management company, with all purchases and sales happening at the market's close. Meanwhile, exchange-traded index funds—often known simply as ETFs—are listed on the stock market, which means they can be bought and sold throughout the trading day. You can invest in ETFs on your own using a discount broker or you can have your financial adviser purchase them for you. In fact, if you use an adviser, ETFs can be an especially fine choice. Even after you figure in the fee paid to your adviser, your total investment bill should still be quite modest, thanks to the low expenses charged by many ETFs.

Indexing has seen explosive growth in recent years, thanks in large part to the popularity of ETFs. Investors and their financial advisers have grudgingly come to accept that the markets are reasonably efficient and that it's extraordinarily difficult to earn market-beating returns. This new-found humility, however, has gone only so far. While many investors now concede that big blue-chip U.S. stocks are efficiently priced, they argue that some markets are less efficient, such as micro-cap U.S. stocks and emerging foreign markets. In theory, savvy investors have an edge in these markets, because the stocks aren't so diligently analyzed and some shares may not reflect all available information. But don't be too quick to buy this argument. In these markets, a big reason for any mispricing is the high cost of trading. In other words, in inefficient markets, winners can be easier to find, but they may be harder to profit from—and thus, buying index mutual funds and ETFs can still be a smart strategy.

## Street Smarts

- Whenever you're tempted to speculate on individual stocks, think about the folks on the other side of the trade and whether you really know more than they do.
- The harder you try to beat the market, the more likely you are to fail, thanks to the investment costs involved.
- If you want to sidestep the risk of badly lagging behind the market, consider index funds—but keep in mind that you will lose money if the underlying indexes perform poorly.

# Chapter Eleven

# Wild Investments Can Tame Our Portfolios

~

*Looking to Zig When
Everything Zags*

Go crazy. You'll feel calmer.

At the end of the last chapter, I mentioned specialized index funds that invest in niche areas like commodities, emerging markets stocks, and real estate investment trusts. These narrowly focused funds can generate both spectacular gains and stomach-churning losses.

Indeed, such "wild" investments are periodically popular with the gambling set, those folks who are gunning for the big win. But forget such nonsense. As I have argued in earlier chapters, you can't forecast returns—but you can control risk. And that, ironically, is a good reason to buy these volatile investments.

## Staying Calm

This might have you scratching your head. How can wild investments help you control risk? As you'll notice from following the markets, investments don't move in lockstep with one another. Sometimes, large-company stocks soar, while small stocks struggle. Sometimes, foreign shares roar ahead, even as U.S. stocks post modest gains. Sometimes, everything gets pummeled, except maybe a single oddball sector. Consider the 2000–2002 collapse, which saw the broad U.S. stock market cut in half. Technology stocks got crushed, but bonds posted offsetting gains—and we got surprisingly good performance from real estate investment trusts and small-company value stocks.

Because different parts of the market don't rise and fall in lockstep with one another, you can reduce your portfolio's overall price gyrations by mixing together these different sectors. When some sectors are sinking, others may be soaring, thus calming down your overall portfolio.

This reduced volatility can be enormously comforting. After all, we may be saving for retirement in 30 years, but we still have to live with our portfolios today. If they're a little calmer, we are more likely to stick with our investments, so we earn the handsome returns that can accrue to long-term investors.

Broad stock-market diversification also delivers benefits over the long haul. Even if you have a decade or more to invest, you can get sharply different results, depending on which parts of the global market you have exposure to. For proof, consider Exhibit 11.1, which shows the relative performance of three market sectors—large U.S. stocks, small U.S. companies, and foreign shares—in the 1970s, 1980s, 1990s, and the first nine years of the new millennium.

**EXHIBIT 11.1  Different Strokes**

*Even over periods as long as a decade, there can be sharp differences in the performance of major stock market sectors.*

|                   | 1970–1979 | 1980–1989 | 1990–1999 | 2000–2008 |
|-------------------|-----------|-----------|-----------|-----------|
| Large U.S. stocks | 5.9%      | 17.6%     | 18.2%     | −3.6%     |
| Small U.S. stocks | 11.5      | 15.8      | 15.1      | 4.1       |
| Foreign stocks    | 8.8       | 22.0      | 7.0       | −1.8      |

*Source:* Ibbotson Associates, a unit of Morningstar, Inc.

*Note:* Performance reflects annualized calendar-year total returns for Standard & Poor's 500, the smallest 20 percent of U.S. stocks as tracked by Ibbotson and Dimensional Fund Advisors, and Morgan Stanley's Europe, Australasia, Far East index.

Among the three sectors, large U.S. stocks ranked third in the 1970s, second in the 1980s, first in the 1990s, and then plunged back to last place in the current decade. Small U.S. stocks ranked first in the 1970s, third in the 1980s, second in the 1990s, and first in the current decade. Meanwhile, foreign stocks were second in the 1970s, first in the 1980s, third in the 1990s, and second in the current decade. In short, all three sectors had their moment in the spotlight—and all three had their decade in the doghouse.

As usual, this comes with a couple of caveats. There's the risk of our portfolio, as reflected in its overall price gyrations, and then there's the risk we perceive. When investing for long-term growth, U.S. investors have tended to favor blue-chip U.S. stocks, those big well-known corporations we know and love. But while these may be comfortable stocks to own, investors can reduce their portfolio's price swings by adding a stake in developed foreign markets and even by venturing into exotic areas like emerging markets, real estate investment trusts, commodities, and gold stocks.

And yet you may not fully appreciate this risk reduction. Take commodities, which can suffer stomach-churning price swings. Because commodities often zig while other investments zag, they may post gains when the rest of your portfolio is slumping, thus helping to trim that year's overall investment loss. The downside: Even if commodities calm down your nest egg's overall volatility, you may not feel any calmer, because you just aren't comfortable owning commodities.

Also, as critics note, a globally diversified portfolio often provides scant comfort during major market melt-downs, when all assets tend to sink simultaneously. But even in this simultaneous sinking, there are often wide varia-tions in performance. In 2008, emerging markets stocks plunged 53 percent, developed foreign markets tumbled 43 percent, blue chip U.S. stocks slumped 37 percent—and small-company value stocks fell 29 percent. Losing 29 percent stings. Still, thanks to that lesser loss, investors got some reward for diversifying widely.

## Spreading It Around

As you look at the widely varying performance of market sectors, over both 1-year and 10-year stretches, there's a dan-ger you forget about risk reduction and instead start pursu-ing performance. This would be a mistake. Unfortunately, in the investment world, the questions that intrigue us most are the ones we're least capable of answering. We all want to know which stocks will skyrocket, where the markets are headed next, what will happen to interest rates, and which mutual fund managers will shine. But as the saying goes,

"If you ask a stupid question, you'll get a stupid answer." Any strategy that involves predicting returns—especially short-term returns—is likely to be a dud, because we just aren't good at forecasting.

What to do? Decide how you will split your money between stocks and conservative investments—or, alternatively, between *growth money* and *safe money*. This will be the key driver of your portfolio's risk and return. Thereafter, forget buying new stock and bond funds for their performance potential. Instead, add a new fund only if you think it will reduce your portfolio's overall risk.

Let's say your goal is to own a mix of roughly 60 percent stocks and 40 percent conservative investments. Start by assuming you will invest your conservative money entirely in a high quality U.S. bond fund. Similarly, begin with the assumption that you will invest all your stock market money in a broad-based U.S. stock fund, such as a U.S. total stock market index fund, which will give you exposure to both large and small U.S. companies. Because you own both stocks and bonds and because you own two broad-based funds, you have already significantly reduced risk.

But you could likely do better. Thanks to the proliferation of mutual funds and exchange-traded index funds, ordinary investors can now build extraordinarily sophisticated portfolios. In fact, you can now put together the sort of investment mix that, until 15 or 20 years ago, was an option for only large institutional investors.

As you strive to lower the risk of your stock portfolio, you might begin by adding a significant stake in a fund that tracks developed foreign markets, so that you have maybe 70 percent of your stock market money in U.S. stocks and 30 percent in foreign markets. You might further tweak this mix by, say, putting a sliver of your foreign stock money into emerging markets and another sliver into small cap stocks from developed foreign markets. In small doses, these investments may reduce your portfolio's overall risk.

Similarly, on the bond side, you might start by dividing your core bond position between conventional high quality U.S. bonds and inflation-indexed Treasury bonds. You might then add small positions in high-yield junk bonds, emerging markets debt, and bonds from developed foreign countries. Again, in small doses, these investments may reduce your portfolio's overall risk.

Alternatively, you might choose to keep your bond investing simple, especially if the bulk of your money is in stocks. Indeed, in building portfolios, a popular strategy is to take risk on the stock side of the portfolio, while playing it relatively safe on the bond side, by sticking with maybe a low-cost short-term bond fund. Historically, short-term bonds have yielded almost as much as long-term bonds, while suffering much less volatility.

Finally, in pursuit of lower portfolio risk, you might take a small portion of the money you've allocated to stocks and bonds and instead devote this money to hard assets. That might mean that your mix of 60 percent stocks and 40 percent bonds becomes maybe 55 percent stocks, 35 percent conservative investments, and 10 percent hard assets, with that 10 percent invested in some combination of commodities, gold stocks, and real estate investment trusts. If you also want some cash investments in the mix, you might carve out a portion of your bond money and stash it in maybe a money market fund.

What would your overall portfolio look like? If your goal is simplicity and you don't want to bother with hard assets, your portfolio might consist of just three funds, with 42 percent in a U.S. total stock market index fund, 18 percent in a broad-based foreign stock index fund and 40 percent in a U.S. total bond market index fund. At the other extreme, if you don't mind complexity, you could purchase a dozen funds and maybe more. For an example of what a more elaborate portfolio might look like, check out Exhibit 11.2.

And, of course, you could always opt for something in between. As you might gather, there's a host of possibilities—and you'll need to figure out what is the right mix for you. Much will depend on how much money

**EXHIBIT 11.2   Slicing and Dicing**

*How many funds you own and what percentage you invest in stocks will hinge on your time horizon, stomach for risk, and tolerance for complexity. Here's what an elaborate balanced portfolio might look like.*

---

*Stocks (55 percent)*
   27 percent U.S. larger companies
   11 percent U.S. smaller companies
   11 percent developed foreign markets
   3 percent international small caps
   3 percent emerging markets

*Hard Assets (10 percent)*
   4 percent real estate investment trusts
   3 percent gold stocks
   3 percent commodities

*Bonds (35 percent)*
   13 percent high quality U.S. bonds
   13 percent inflation-indexed Treasuries
   3 percent high yield junk bonds
   3 percent developed foreign markets
   3 percent emerging markets debt

---

you have to invest, how much hassle you're willing to endure, and how comfortable you are with more exotic parts of the global financial markets.

## Keeping Our Balance

I am often asked what percentage of a stock portfolio should be allocated to foreign stocks. Should it be 25 or 30 percent? And what about emerging markets debt?

Should it be 5 percent of the bond portfolio—or maybe 10 percent? My standard answer: Within reason, the precise percentages are far less important than your willingness to stick with them. Over the long haul, it won't much matter if you have 8 or 12 percent of your overall portfolio in hard assets. But if you go for 12 percent and sell in a panic when hard assets get roughed up, you will badly damage your results. You want portfolio percentages you'll stick with—in good times and bad.

Once you have settled on which market sectors you will buy and in what amounts, write down your target percentages. At times of market turmoil, your written targets will remind you of the plan you settled on in calmer times. These targets are the investment policy that guides both your basic asset allocation among stocks, bonds, hard assets, and cash investments and also your strategy for diversifying within these broad categories.

Thereafter, every year or so, check how your current mix compares to your target percentages and then possibly rebalance, a strategy discussed back in Chapter Seven. As you might recall, rebalancing between stocks and more conservative investments can keep your portfolio's risk level under control. The idea is to invest more in stocks when they fall below your target percentage and lighten up when they're flying high.

But you may also want to rebalance within your stocks, within your hard assets, and within your bonds—and this has the potential to both control risk and boost returns. Consider U.S. and foreign stocks. Over the past four decades, they have generated similar long-run returns. So why own foreign shares? U.S. and foreign stocks fare well at different times, so holding both will give you a portfolio with lower overall volatility. There is, however, a bonus. You may, through rebalancing, be able to profit from their differing pattern of returns.

The notion: You set target portfolio percentages for U.S. and foreign stocks and then regularly tweak your portfolio to bring it back into line with these targets. This will force you to buy in to the sector that is suffering and ease up on the one that's faring well. This buy low–sell high strategy should boost your portfolio's long-run performance, assuming U.S. and foreign stocks generate similar returns over the long haul.

As I mentioned in Chapter Seven, rebalancing is best done within a retirement account. If you are regularly selling winning investments held in your taxable account, the resulting capital gains tax bill will eat into any profit from rebalancing. You may still want to rebalance to keep your portfolio's risk level under control—but your after-tax performance will pay the price.

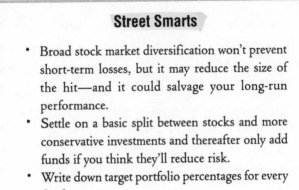

### Street Smarts

- Broad stock market diversification won't prevent short-term losses, but it may reduce the size of the hit—and it could salvage your long-run performance.
- Settle on a basic split between stocks and more conservative investments and thereafter only add funds if you think they'll reduce risk.
- Write down target portfolio percentages for every fund you own.

# Chapter Twelve

# Short-Term Results Matter to Long-Term Investors

~

*Keep One Eye on the Horizon—And the Other on the Ground Ahead*

WHENEVER STOCKS TAKE A BEATING, investors are advised to remain calm. "Stay the course," counsel the pundits. "If you've got a long time to invest, this sort of market craziness just doesn't matter."

That, however, isn't entirely true. Sure, you might have nerves of steel, so you aren't inclined to panic. Yes, rotten market returns should eventually be followed by stretches of good performance, as economic growth propels share prices higher.

But what happens in the short term is still hugely important to your long-run results.

## Retiring to Monte Carlo

There are two issues here. First, truly terrible returns can have a devastating impact on investment compounding, thanks to the brutal math of investing. If you lose 10 percent, it takes an 11 percent gain to get back to even. Give up 20 percent and you're looking at a 25 percent rebound to recoup your losses. What if you lose 50 percent? To make yourself whole, you need a 100 percent gain.

All this is yet another reason to own a broad array of stocks, including some of the wild investments mentioned in the last chapter, and to hold at least some bonds. That won't stop you from losing money. But it should mute your losses and thus make it easier to recover. Indeed, to the extent you can smooth out your year-to-year returns and avoid big losses, your portfolio's compounding will become much more efficient.

To appreciate why, imagine two portfolios, one that returns 8 percent every year and the other that alternates between climbing 32 percent one year and sinking 16 percent the next. If you simply add up the individual annual returns for the two portfolios over a 10-year stretch, you get a total of 80 percent in both cases. But 80 percent isn't the right answer, because it ignores the way money grows over time, with each year's gains or losses building on top of the prior performance. If you figure in this investment compounding, you find the steady performer earned a cumulative 116 percent over the 10 years, while the erratic performer notched just 68 percent.

What's the second issue? You need to consider how your portfolio's performance intersects with your own buying and selling. Suppose you are in your twenties and starting to save for retirement. You might like the idea of investing a few bucks in the stock market and immediately seeing your newly acquired shares soar in value. But if you really want to get rich, you should pray for decades of miserable results followed by a huge bull market just before you retire. That way, you will buy shares at beaten-down prices and then, if all goes well, cash out at lofty valuations.

On the other hand, if you're unlucky, you will get miserable stock market returns just as you quit the workforce. Consider the treacherous situation confronting those who retired at the start of 2000 or the start of 2008. While a big market decline can have a silver lining if you're still working, because you can use your monthly savings to buy shares at lower prices, there is no silver lining once you retire. Instead of buying stocks, you're looking to sell. In fact, if you have just retired, your nest egg may be as plump as it's ever been—and a bear market could mean a huge hit in dollar terms. The danger: A combination of the market's decline and your own need for spending money could put a big dent in your portfolio's value and your nest egg may never recover, leaving you to pinch pennies for the rest of your days.

Because of this so-called sequence-of-return risk, many experts have stopped making financial projections using average rates of return. Instead, they use models that employ a technique known as Monte Carlo analysis, which involves testing a strategy in hundreds or even thousands of different market scenarios. If you're playing around with the retirement calculators available on the Internet, pay careful attention to what rates of return are assumed—and whether the calculator uses Monte Carlo analysis or just average returns.

## Cushioning with Cash

How can you cope with sequence-of-return risk? If you're still in the workforce, it is easy enough. As discussed in earlier chapters, you should regularly rebalance your portfolio, so you buy low and sell high. You may also want to step up your buying whenever stocks take a big hit. Between rebalancing, extra buying, and reinvesting dividends, you can turn market declines into a potential money-making opportunity.

For retirees, things are trickier. The goal: Reduce the risk of devastating losses—and try not to sell stocks during tumbling markets. To sidestep devastating losses, focus on diversifying broadly and keeping maybe half your portfolio in conservative investments. Meanwhile, to avoid selling stocks during big market declines, think carefully about where your spending money will come from.

To pay the bills in retirement, you will have your monthly Social Security check and any pension and annuity income. But there is a chance you can't cover all your living expenses with these sources alone. Instead, you may need to pull money from your portfolio. To make sure you can do that without having to sell stocks at distressed prices, figure out how much spending money you will need from your portfolio over the next five years.

Let's say you are using a 5 percent portfolio withdrawal rate. This represents the percentage of your portfolio's value that you pull out in the first year of retirement. Thereafter, the assumption is that you would step up the sum with inflation. In other words, if you retired with $300,000, used a 5 percent withdrawal rate and inflation ran at 3 percent, you would pull out $15,000 in year one,

$15,450 in year two, $15,914 in year three and so on. This 5 percent draw would come not only from your portfolio's dividends and interest, but also from occasionally selling stocks and bonds.

In practice, almost nobody follows this strategy. We tend to spend more when our investments are faring well and cut back when markets are suffering. Our spending in retirement may also decline over time, as we grow less active, though it could suddenly surge if we're hit with hefty medical or long-term care expenses.

Still, let's assume you are using the 5 percent withdrawal strategy or something similar, which means you will spend a sum equal to roughly 25 percent of your portfolio's value over the next five years. Take this 25 percent, designate it as your "cash cushion," and invest it in conservative investments like short-term bond funds, money market funds, and certificates of deposit. That will cover you for the next five years—and free you up to invest the other 75 percent of your portfolio more aggressively. With this 75 percent, you might put 25 percent in a mix of U.S. and foreign bonds with attractive yields and most of the remaining 50 percent in stocks, with perhaps a smidgen in hard assets.

Each year, dip into your cash cushion for the spending money you need from your portfolio. Meanwhile, to replenish your cash cushion, direct all dividends, interest, and mutual fund distributions into, say, your money market fund. If the markets fare well in any given year, also sell a little of your stock portfolio and other riskier investments. Move the proceeds into your money market fund, so that you keep your cash cushion at 25 percent of your portfolio's total value. What if the stock market slumps and riskier bonds get beaten up? Hold off all sales until these markets recover. With five years of spending money in your cash cushion, you could ride out a long bear market without selling any of your riskier investments.

---

### Street Smarts

- By building a portfolio that is unlikely to suffer big short-term losses, you should improve your long-run investment compounding.
- If you're saving for retirement, you shouldn't fear stock market declines, but instead welcome them as opportunities.
- In retirement, hold a cash reserve equal to maybe five years' spending money, so you reduce the risk you'll need to sell stocks during a bear market.

# A Long Life Is a Big Risk

---

## *The Danger: We Run out of Money Before We Run out of Breath*

LIVE LONG AND PROSPER. Maybe.

Drawing down a portfolio in retirement is one of life's trickiest financial conundrums. We don't know what the inflation rate will be and what surprise expenses we will face. We don't know what long-run returns we'll earn and when the next bear market will hit.

On top of all this, there's another big uncertainty: We don't know how long we will live—and that means it is hard to gauge how much money we can safely pull from our nest egg each year. Withdraw too much and we could outlive our savings. Withdraw too little and we may spend our retirement scrimping unnecessarily.

What to do? Welcome to the world of longevity risk.

## Outliving the Averages

Life expectancy can be a tad confusing. Some folks look at life expectancies as of birth. But such averages are dragged down by those who die before they reach retirement age. Instead, if you're thinking about spending down a portfolio in retirement, you want to focus on life expectancy as of age 65. Today, a 65-year-old man can expect to live until age 83, while a 65-year-old woman can expect to live until age 85.

But even these numbers are misleading, because they are just averages. Not only will half of retirees live longer, there's also a huge variation around these averages. Some people will die in their late sixties or early seventies, while a sizable minority will make it to age 90. Moreover, if you are married, you're dealing with two life expectancies—which means there is a good chance that at least one of you will live beyond your life expectancy. Also, keep in

mind that the averages reflect the general U.S. popula-
tion. What about well-educated, affluent folks who
exercise regularly, don't smoke, drink in moderation, and
read personal finance books? They will likely live longer
than average. The bottom line: Unless you are in poor
health when you retire, you should probably err on the
side of caution and plan for a retirement that extends to
age 90 and maybe beyond.

To complicate matters, there is inflation. At 3 percent
a year, the spending power of a dollar is cut in half in just
23 years, which means the fixed pension you receive at
age 65 will buy just half as much at age 88. And, if anything, this understates the problem. The general standard
of living rises not with inflation, but with per capita
economic growth, which typically climbs some two percentage points a year faster than inflation.

This is why retirees often feel pinched even if their
incomes are keeping pace with inflation. Incidentally, this is
also why it's so hard to keep family fortunes intact. After
income is distributed to family members and taxes are paid, it
is unlikely a family fortune will grow very much over the
long haul, yet alone match the rate of per capita economic
growth. And if a family fortune isn't maintaining pace with
per capita economic growth, it can't kick off income over
the long haul that will allow family members to keep up
with the general standard of living.

## Making It Last

So how can you arrange a retirement income stream that rises over time and that lasts at least as long as you do? The precise strategy you settle on will depend on a fistful of factors, including your appetite for risk, whether you have a pension, how much you have saved, whether you are married, your current health and likely longevity, and whether you're looking to leave behind a substantial estate. Still, as you design your strategy, keep in mind some key notions.

For starters, forget the traditional approach favored by retirees, which is to buy bonds and live off the income. That will leave you vulnerable to inflation, as the spending power of both your interest income and your bonds' principal value is gradually eroded. To counteract inflation, you need to reinvest part of your annual investment gain back into your portfolio during the early years of retirement, so that your nest egg's growth comes close to rivaling inflation.

The trouble is, if you are investing entirely in bonds, certificates of deposit, and other conservative investments, this need to reinvest likely won't leave you with much money to spend. Indeed, this is why you should seriously consider holding some stock funds, so you have a shot at earning healthy, inflation-beating gains. Sure, this is risky. But you can manage the risk with the cash cushion strategy described in the previous chapter.

While holding stocks can make retirees nervous, they often have plenty of time to ride out rough markets. Retirement isn't a hard deadline, like buying a home or paying for college. You might spend down your portfolio over 30 years—and your investment time horizon may even extend beyond your lifetime. Suppose you are age 65. If you plan to bequeath part of your portfolio to your children or grandchildren, you might be dealing with a 50- or 80-year time horizon. It's hard to imagine stocks wouldn't generate handsome gains over that long a time frame.

To counteract inflation and ensure you have a healthy amount of income, also consider delaying Social Security. You can claim Social Security retirement benefits as early as age 62 or as late as age 70. The longer you delay, the larger your monthly check will be. In fact, if Social Security remains in its current form and isn't cut back, it may prove to be your most valuable retirement asset. After all, it's government guaranteed, inflation-linked, at least partially tax-free and you get it for life. In addition, Social Security comes with both a spousal benefit and a survivor's benefit. Suppose you were the family's breadwinner. Even if you are in poor health, you may want to delay claiming Social Security to get a larger monthly benefit because your spouse will likely receive your benefit as a survivor benefit. In effect, the life expectancy of your Social Security benefit is longer than your own life expectancy.

If you have a pension, that will give you another source of lifetime income. No pension? To supplement Social Security, you might sink part of your nest egg into an immediate fixed annuity that pays lifetime income. A lifetime income annuity typically doesn't have any principal value. Instead, all it gives you is a stream of regular income for as long as you live. Cast your mind back to the strategy discussed in Chapter Twelve. Let's say you earmarked 25 percent of your savings for a cash cushion and another 50 percent for stock funds. That leaves 25 percent. As suggested in Chapter Twelve, you could put this 25 percent in higher-yielding U.S. and foreign bonds—or, alternatively, you might invest it in a lifetime income annuity.

The annuity will likely give you more income than the bonds, and the annuity's stream of income is guaranteed for life. Many folks dislike immediate annuities because they fear they will die early in retirement and the money they sunk into the annuity will be gone. Still, if your nest egg is on the small side, an immediate annuity may be a good bet if you need a healthy amount of income.

If you aren't keen on buying an annuity, you might instead take maybe 20 percent of your nest egg at age 65 and set it aside to grow until age 85. Think of this as your financial backstop in case you live a surprisingly long time. In the meantime, you can spend down the other 80 percent between now and age 85. If you die before age 85, the 20 percent will go to your heirs, along with any other savings you have left. What if you live to age 85? At that juncture, you will have a choice. If your health is shaky, you could spend down the 20 percent you set aside. But if your health remains robust, you might use these savings to buy an immediate annuity that pays lifetime income. Because of your advanced age, the annuity should offer a handsome monthly payout. Need additional income? If you own your home, you could always tap into its value through a reverse mortgage.

## Street Smarts

- Unless your health is poor, plan on a retirement that lasts until age 90—and maybe longer.
- To give yourself more guaranteed lifetime income, consider delaying Social Security and thereby getting a larger monthly check.
- If you want to lock up additional lifetime income, look into immediate fixed annuities.

# Chapter Fourteen

# Markets May Be Rational, but We Aren't

❧

## Investing Is Simple—And Yet It Sure Isn't Easy

SENSIBLE MONEY MANAGEMENT is pretty straightforward: We need to save regularly, control risk, buy a few funds, hold down costs, and keep half an eye on taxes. As I hope I've made clear in the preceding chapters, investing can be remarkably simple.

And yet it sure isn't easy. We make all kinds of behavioral mistakes, including saving too little, growing overconfident as markets rise, and losing faith when share prices tumble. That doesn't mean we all make the same mental mistakes and share the same behavioral quirks. But some of these quirks are pretty widespread—and they hurt many folks' investment results.

All this represents a partial repudiation of classical economics, which assumes our behavior is rational. Rational? Think about that next time you fail to go to the gym, eat the chocolate you swore you wouldn't touch, spend too much at the mall, and once again rack up shocking credit card bills.

## Struggling to Save

Indeed, our behavioral struggles start with our lack of self-control, which means we find it tough to delay gratification and we end up saving far too little. As I suggested in Chapter Four, this may have evolutionary roots. Our hunter–gatherer ancestors didn't give much thought to how they would pay for retirement. Instead, they were focused on surviving, which meant consuming whenever they could. Maybe it is no great surprise that delaying gratification doesn't come easily to us today—and why we need to engage in all kinds of trickery to get ourselves to save.

As a substitute for trickery, you might imagine that we could try financial education. The trouble is, education doesn't appear to work. We all know we need to save, but we still fall short. For instance, if we are asked whether—starting a year from now—we would be willing to cut out some luxuries and thereby save an extra $100 a week, we might say, "Yes." But if we're asked whether we would be willing to start the belt-tightening immediately, we would likely balk. We know what is good for us in the long term but, because it is the long term, it is easy to procrastinate. Like the sinner's prayer, "God save me—but not yet."

While a lack of self-control is probably the biggest reason we don't save enough, we can also blame our profligate ways on our inadequate math skills. Most of us don't carry around financial calculators. Instead, when confronted with everyday financial math problems, we guess—and our guesses usually aren't very good. For instance, we may be aware of the effects of compounding, the process by which we earn investment gains not only on our original investment, but also on the gains earned in earlier years that we reinvested back into our nest egg.

But while we have some sense for how compounding works, we tend to underestimate its impact. That means we don't realize how much our savings could grow over time and thus we aren't as motivated to save as we should be. By the same token, we underestimate how much our debts are costing us. We may know that our credit cards charge a steep interest rate, but we don't fully appreciate how much interest we will incur if we fail to pay off our credit cards in full. Every month we carry a card balance, we get charged interest on that unpaid balance. It is like investing, except that time is our enemy, not our friend.

## Riding the Bull

If saving is a battle, investing is a war—and many of our wounds are self-inflicted. Imagine we're in the early stages of a stock market rally. At that juncture, our inclination is to be too conservative. As behavioral economists have discovered, we tend to be loss averse, getting far more pain from losses than pleasure from gains. In fact, academic studies suggest our pain from losses is twice as great as the pleasure we get from gains.

During the stock market's initial recovery, this loss aversion can cause us to shy away from stocks. We may have heard about the market's great long-run gains. But we are much more focused on the possibility of terrible short-term losses. We hate the idea that we'll dump a bunch of money into stocks just to see the market plunge. That would mean wretched losses—and terrible pangs of regret.

This helps explain the popularity of dollar-cost averaging, the strategy of investing the same sum every month no matter what. Dollar-cost averaging is trumpeted as a disciplined, no-nonsense approach to buying stocks. But it's really about investor psychology, helping us to overcome our reluctance to invest and making market declines seem more palatable. Sure, this month's investment may turn out to be a money loser. But we have the comfort of knowing that next month we'll get another chance to buy.

As the market continues to climb, we grow a little more willing to purchase stocks. But as we consider what to buy, academic research suggests we will likely favor the familiar. Many folks appear to suffer from *home bias,* meaning we tend to favor our employer's shares, local companies, well-known blue-chip stocks and corporations whose products we use. Combined together, such stocks may create a poorly diversified portfolio—and yet this is the portfolio we're comfortable owning.

Meanwhile, we shy away from exotic fare like commodities and foreign stocks, even though these exotic investments may damp down our portfolio's overall volatility. As the rally gathers steam, however, such exotic investments may start to seem less risky, especially if they're posting big gains. We are hardwired to search for patterns, teasing out all kinds of confident forecasts from the market's chaotic gyrations. This search for patterns causes us to extrapolate recent returns and, before long, we're assuming that the rising market will keep on rising. Forget the long sweep of history. We are much more heavily influenced by what's happened in recent weeks and months.

Pretty soon, we have forgotten all the uncertainty about the market's direction. Instead, we convince ourselves that it was obvious stocks were going to climb. We may even decide that we foresaw the rally. This *hindsight bias* makes the market seem more predictable than it really is and we're emboldened to pursue our current investment hunches.

The high-flying market also bolsters our confidence, as we attribute our investment gains to our own brilliance, and we become enthralled with beating the market. That leads us to make bigger investment bets and buy actively managed funds. Men are—surprise, surprise—especially susceptible to all this, tending to trade more, stash more in stocks, and pursue riskier stock investment strategies.

We may even fall prey to the *house money* effect. Like casino gamblers who get lucky early in the evening, our investment success may make us feel like we're ahead of the game—and we can afford to take extra risk. True, there may be warning signs, including rich valuations and naysaying pundits. But we disregard contradictory information and pay scant attention to statistical data. Instead, we latch on to those arguments, anecdotes, and other scraps of evidence that bolster our position.

Taking our cues from the work world, we associate hard work with success. More research and more trading feels like it should lead to superior results. Sure enough, some of our stocks rise and we take immense satisfaction in turning our paper profits into hard cash. The problem is, selling winners not only triggers investment costs, but also it can mean big tax bills if we're trading in a taxable account.

Money, however, is only part of the payoff. Forget about achieving goals. Wall Street becomes entertainment. We love the feeling that we're in the flow of the market's action. We get a thrill from buying and selling. Trading makes us feel emotionally engaged with our money and it gives us a sense of control. We start to identify with our investments. We're proud when we are allocated 100 shares of a hot initial public stock offering. We like the cachet that comes with owning a hedge fund. We buy socially responsible mutual funds, touting our ownership as a sign of our political commitment.

Early in the rally, trading rapidly and buying exotic securities would have seemed risky. Now, it feels almost safe, in part because plenty of others are doing the same. We flock to popular investments, taking comfort in the validation we get from those around us. Popularity, of course, is often a good sign when picking a movie, a car, or a restaurant. But in the investment world, crowds are dangerous. If an investment is highly popular, there is a good chance it is overpriced. Once everybody has bought, there is no one left to buy. The next bear market? It probably isn't too far away.

## Losing Our Nerve

Market rallies often last far longer than skeptics expect. Bearish investors declare that the end is nigh, only to see skyrocketing share prices make a mockery of their forecasts. But eventually, as mother predicted, "it'll end in tears." Whenever an investment becomes wildly popular, you can be fairly sure rough times lie ahead—even if you can't be certain when those bad times will hit.

When stocks first falter, we shrug it off. But as the slide continues, our confidence slips away. We're no longer so sure about our predictions and we aren't so inclined to trade. Instead of extrapolating endless gains, we now assume the market will continue to fall. Some, fearing further losses, hit the panic button and sell. But many folks simply freeze. We tend to regret errors of commission more than errors of omission. It's bad enough that we are losing money. But if we make another trade and it doesn't pan out, we will feel even worse.

As we bite our nails and sit tight, we are influenced by the endowment effect, the tendency to look beyond market prices and impute additional value to the things we own. This is the reason we hang on to the stocks we inherited from our parents, we think our portfolios have fared better than they really have and we believe our investments and our homes are worth more than the current market price.

Similarly, as we mentally value our stocks and our stock funds, we might also be anchored off the price we paid or the price we could have got if we had sold at the market peak—and we are profoundly reluctant to sell for less. Experts talk about risk aversion. But in truth, we are loss averse. We loathe the idea of losing money. In fact, we will hang on to a risky, badly diversified portfolio, praying we can "get even, then get out." Selling means giving up all chance of recouping our losses and admitting we made a mistake. We might even "double down" on losing stock positions, buying more shares and taking more risk in the hope that this will help us recoup our losses more quickly.

It won't necessarily be our stocks that cause us the most distress. We expect stocks to perform erratically. Instead, we can become especially unnerved if supposedly safe investments turn out to be risky. We aren't much bothered by a 1 percent stock market decline. But we are alarmed by the idea that the $1 share price of our money market fund might "break the buck" and fall to 99 cents.

Loss aversion isn't such a bad thing. It could, during a bear market, prevent us from selling at the worst possible time. If we own well-diversified portfolios, it's probably good that we hang on to the investments we have. But we would likely fare even better if, instead of freezing, we were buying more shares as prices declined. Market declines are opportunities. Unfortunately, for many, they are an opportunity to make yet more mistakes.

As with our struggles to save, many of our financial errors can be traced to evolutionary psychology. Our ancestors survived because they worked hard, hunted for patterns, mimicked others, and greatly feared losses. But these traits can hurt us in the modern financial world. Forget blaming everything on our parents. The real culprits, it seems, are our cave-dwelling ancestors.

## Getting a Grip

What's the solution to all this? With any luck, a little self-knowledge will help us avoid some pitfalls. If we keep in mind our many mental mistakes and we strive to stay focused on the economic fundamentals mentioned in Chapter Eight, maybe we'll act a little more sensibly and maybe we'll approach the markets with a little more humility.

Still, just as we manipulated ourselves so we saved more, we might also need to trick ourselves into better investment behavior. Standard financial theory tells us to build well-diversified portfolios and then focus on the risk and return of the overall portfolio. But many folks find that hard to do, fretting instead over the performance of each investment they own. If you're in that camp, you may want to favor investments that wrap together a slew of different market sectors into one portfolio.

Many 401(k) plans, recognizing that employees often struggle to invest intelligently, are doing just that. They have added what are called *life cycle funds, target-date retirement funds,* or *lifestyle funds* to their plan's menu of investment choices. These funds offer one-stop investment shopping, combining a bunch of market sectors in a single mutual fund. Within the fund, some sectors may be flying high and others getting trashed. But all shareholders see is a single share price that performs relatively sedately.

Simply adding such funds to a 401(k) isn't enough, however. The problem: Many employees don't bother contributing to their 401(k) and, if they do, they don't bother picking investments. To overcome this not-so-benign neglect, some companies are now automatically enrolling employees in their 401(k) and they have designated these one-stop-shopping funds as their plan's default investment option. Employees can always choose not to enroll and they can usually pick other investments. But inertia is a powerful force—and many employees don't opt out, which means they end up saving more and investing more sensibly than they otherwise would.

In Chapter Six, I mentioned the idea of mentally dividing your nest egg into *growth money* and *safe money.* You may also want to add a third category, *fun money.* Slice off

3 or 5 percent of your portfolio and use that to trade and buy wild-and-crazy investments. You probably won't make much money. But the damage will, at least, be confined to a relatively small portion of your portfolio. One warning: Before you set up a fun-money account, make sure you're on track for retirement and other goals—and that your fun-money losses won't derail these plans.

If you often torpedo your own investment results, also consider hiring a financial adviser. View the adviser's role as that of a coach, somebody to encourage you to save regularly, diversify broadly, hang tough at times of market turbulence, and make smarter decisions in other areas of your financial life. The adviser is there to nudge you toward better financial behavior and away from self-inflicted investment wounds. Your adviser may not earn you market-beating results—but he could help you capture more of the market's return, so you don't lag badly behind the market averages.

Even with an adviser's handholding, you may find it tough to cope with the market's craziness. But perhaps your fears will subside over time. Our tolerance for risk may rise and fall along with the markets. But it also changes with experience. Younger investors are supposedly more risk tolerant—and that's certainly true in regard to their time horizon. But when it comes to mental toughness, the advantage may go to older investors who have lived through some market cycles and know what to expect. A 25-year-old with 60 percent in stocks may be terrified as share prices plunge—and a 65-year-old with the same portfolio may be entirely comfortable. Feeling unnerved? Maybe you need to give it time.

---

### Street Smarts

- Resist following the crowd, whether it's chasing hot performers in bull markets or shunning stocks during market declines.
- If you agonize over each investment you own, consider mutual funds that provide one-stop investment shopping.
- Unnerved by tumbling share prices? Tempted to overhaul your entire portfolio? Get a second opinion from a friend, a colleague, or your financial adviser.

# Chapter Fifteen

# Our Homes Are a Fine Investment that Won't Appreciate Much

~

## *They're Money Pits—with Impressive Dividends*

THERE'S NO PLACE LIKE HOME, but not for the reason people think.

Even with the housing market's sometimes wild price swings, many folks are convinced that buying a home is the best investment they can make. In fact, real estate is so popular that, when people reach retirement age, their home typically accounts for half of the wealth they have accumulated.

Yet, if you dig into the numbers, you discover that homes usually aren't a great way to make your money grow. But don't despair: They can still be a mighty fine investment.

## Mortgaging Our Future

Confused? Let's start with the dismal history of home-price appreciation. Over the 30 years through year-end 2008, home prices climbed an average 4.7 percent a year, according to home finance corporation Freddie Mac. That's barely ahead of inflation, which ran at 3.8 percent a year. Moreover, homeownership comes with all kinds of expenses that you don't incur as a renter, including property taxes, maintenance costs, and homeowner's insurance. Those costs could easily amount to 3 percent or more of your home's value each year. Subtract that from the 30-year average price gain of 4.7 percent and homeowners aren't even keeping pace with inflation.

This shouldn't be any great surprise. Yes, the land underneath your home ought to appreciate modestly in value. After all, as the old saw goes, they aren't making any more of it. But the roof over your head and the four walls that surround you are, arguably, a depreciating asset that—without a lot of love and a lot of dollars—will likely lose value. For proof, consider the lackluster financial return from making home improvements.

Many people think of remodeling as investing in their home. But if you fix up your home and then try to sell, studies suggest you will recoup only a portion of the money you spent. Like the sofa in your living room and the chairs around the dining room table, your remodeling projects never again look as good as they did on that first day. Slowly, these improvements deteriorate, the nicks and scratches pile up and, soon enough, it is time to spruce up your house again.

So why do homeowners often claim that their home is the best investment they ever made? There may be two reasons. First, even modest annual price gains can appear impressive, given enough time and enough investment compounding. If you conveniently forget the hefty costs of homeownership and focus solely on the 4.7 percent annual gain, you're looking at almost 300 percent price appreciation over 30 years.

Second, many homeowners take out a mortgage when they purchase a home and that can make their profit appear even larger. A 300 percent price gain over 30 years, from maybe $100,000 to $400,000, sounds good. But it would appear even more spectacular if you had put down, say, $20,000 initially and walked away with $400,000 after 30 years. You anted up just 20 percent of the purchase price and borrowed the other 80 percent. But because you're the owner, you enjoy the full fruits of any price appreciation. A mortgage, in effect, leverages a home's price gain.

The problem is, this leverage can make your entire finances more perilous—a topic discussed in Chapter One. It can also aggravate losses during real estate downturns, as folks discovered during the slump that began in mid-2006. This sort of brutal price decline can quickly wipe out your home equity, so that your home is worth less than the sum owed on your mortgage. Because the combination of tumbling home prices and borrowed money is so treacherous, you shouldn't buy a home unless you can see staying put for at least five years and preferably seven years or longer.

Even when home prices climb, leverage is a mixed blessing. In the first few years that you own a home, when you have relatively little home equity and a lot of mortgage debt, you could potentially benefit big-time from leverage. For instance, if you put down $50,000 on a $250,000 house and your home appreciates to $300,000, your home equity would double from $50,000 to $100,000.

This profit, however, is less impressive than it seems. Yes, in the early years of your mortgage, you stand to benefit the most from leveraged gains, because you have relatively little home equity and a lot of debt. But this is also the time when you're paying the most interest each year and that interest should be set against any price gains.

Indeed, there is a chance that your mortgage interest rate is greater than your home's annual price appreciation, so the leverage is working against you. The good news is, as your monthly mortgage payments whittle down your loan balance, thus paying more of your home's original purchase price, you will fork over less in total interest each year. But that also means you won't enjoy those spectacular leveraged gains, because you now have less mortgage debt outstanding. Eventually, you might pay off your mortgage entirely—at which point there's no leverage and your home-price appreciation might look like Freddie Mac's pedestrian 4.7 percent average annual gain.

To make matters worse, it isn't just mortgage interest, property taxes, homeowner's insurance, and maintenance costs that eat into the return from homeownership. You also need to take into account the hefty costs involved in first buying a home and later selling it. In particular, you could lose a big chunk of your gain to the 5 or 6 percent commission that the selling real estate brokerage firm might charge. Just sold your home for $500,000? The brokers involved might be looking at a $25,000 or $30,000 payday.

## Collecting the Rent

Even with all these costs, however, homes can still be a great investment. Forget price appreciation. Think instead about the imputed rent. As with stocks, bonds, and other investments, you can break down a house's total return into its capital gain and its dividend. A home's capital gain may be modest and largely offset by the costs involved. But the dividend is huge. Consider how much you might earn if you rented out your house. Conceivably, you could receive a sum each year equal to 7 or 8 percent of your home's current market price. That is an indication of how much value you get from your house, as you live there rent-free.

Of course, you might feel you don't get all that much value from your home and that you could get more by renting it out. This can happen if you own a property that's bigger than you really need. The lesson: Be sure to buy a house that is the right size for you and your family—and no larger. That way, you won't be wasting rent by owning a place that is too large. Instead, you could take the money you didn't sink into the big house and invest it elsewhere, where it will likely earn better returns.

There's an added advantage to living in your own home and enjoying its imputed rent. Unlike the dividends and interest from your investments, you don't have to pay taxes on this imputed rent. This tax-free benefit is on top of the better-known tax breaks that homeowners enjoy, including the ability to take a tax deduction for mortgage interest and property taxes and to avoid capital gains taxes on a big chunk of the profit when selling a home.

People may also behave a little more sensibly with their homes than with, say, their stocks. Real estate speculation occasionally gets out of hand, and it was especially bad in 2005 and 2006. Still, you typically don't see the long litany of mistakes that you see in the financial markets and which I described in Chapter Fourteen. Possible explanations: We don't get the daily price information we get with stocks, we can't so easily sell our homes—and we've got to live somewhere. That means homeowners are less likely to sell in a panic during times of real estate turmoil. Instead, they hang on through the downturns, they keep making those monthly mortgage payments, they slowly pay down their loan balance, and they build up home equity. One day, the mortgage is paid off, a hefty monthly cost is eliminated and, lo and behold, they own a major asset free and clear.

## Street Smarts

- Aim to buy a home that's the right size for you and your family—and no larger.
- Before purchasing a house, make sure you will stay put for at least five years and preferably longer.
- Don't expect impressive price gains from your home, especially once you figure in the hefty costs of homeownership.

*Chapter Sixteen*

# Paying off Debts Could Be Our Best Bond Investment

—— ∾ ——

*How Does a Guaranteed
15 Percent Sound?*

MAYBE IT'S TIME TO LOSE INTEREST.

Our top savings priority is pretty clear: If our employer provides a 401(k) with a matching contribution, we ought to be socking away at least enough to get the full employer match. That employer match, after all, is free money.

Also, a conventional 401(k) offers an initial tax deduction and tax-deferred growth, plus the chance to earn investment gains.

Once we've funded the 401(k), however, the choices get trickier—and sometimes paying down debt is the best investment we can make. This might have you scratching your head. Shouldn't we keep our spending and borrowing separate from our saving and investing? Not at all. It's true that one is about consumption today and the other is about consumption tomorrow. But they are all part of our financial life—and they're all connected.

## Going Negative

If you recall from Chapter One, our net worth is our total assets, including our mutual funds, bank accounts, and real estate, minus our debts. If we save $300 this month, but we also add $300 to our credit card balance, we haven't made any financial progress. And if the $300 we saved earns 2 percent in a money market account while our credit card balance is costing us 15 percent, we're losing ground.

Want to increase your net worth? After you have stashed enough in your 401(k) to get the full employer match, your next best investment may be paying off those credit cards that are costing you 15 percent. By paying down your cards, you will reduce your debts and hence increase your net worth. As an added bonus, the effective return from paying down your cards is a guaranteed 15 percent. In some years, you may earn more than 15 percent in the stock market. But it certainly isn't guaranteed.

In fact, you can think of paying down debt as a conservative investment strategy, not unlike buying high quality bonds. As I suggested in Chapter One, you might even view your debts as negative bonds. While your bonds pay you interest, your debts are costing you interest. And that cost can be pretty steep. As you might have noticed, you are considered less creditworthy than, say, the federal government. That means you will typically pay a higher interest rate when you borrow. Indeed, the interest rate you pay on your mortgage, student loans, credit card balances, and auto loans is likely higher than the interest rate you earn on the high quality bonds you own. The implication: If you're in a mood to buy bonds, you may be better off paying down your debts.

## Shedding Debts

Like funding a 401(k) with an employer match, paying off high-cost credit card debt is pretty much a no-brainer. Both can offer an impressive return on your money. But should you pay off your other debts as well? Much depends on what interest rate you're charged on those debts, whether the interest is tax-deductible, and what other investment options are open to you.

Let's say that, after you paid off your credit cards, the only debt you have left is your 30-year fixed-rate mortgage that is costing 6 percent. You are able to deduct that mortgage interest on your federal tax return. Meanwhile, high quality taxable bonds are yielding 5 percent. Should you buy the high quality taxable bonds or pay down your mortgage? The answer depends, in part, on which account you'll use to buy the 5 percent bonds.

If you purchase the bonds in, say, a tax-deductible individual retirement account, you will get both an initial tax deduction and tax-deferred growth. That will likely make buying the bonds more attractive than paying down your 6 percent mortgage. Sure, the mortgage carries a higher interest rate. But if you're in, say, the 25 percent federal income tax bracket and you itemize your tax deductions, the after-tax cost of your mortgage is just 4.5 percent—and thus you should earn more by buying the 5 percent bonds in the tax-favored IRA.

On the other hand, if the choice is between paying down your 6 percent mortgage and buying the 5 percent bonds in your regular taxable account, you would probably want to pay down your mortgage. Yes, the after-tax cost of the mortgage is just 4.5 percent. But after you have paid income taxes on the interest from your 5 percent bonds, you will be left with just 3.75 percent.

All of this discussion assumes that you're a conservative investor choosing between paying down your mortgage and buying high quality taxable bonds. But if you're a more aggressive investor, your taste runs to stocks, and you have taxable account money to invest, you should probably skip the extra principal payments on your mortgage and buy stocks instead. Even after paying taxes on your stock market gains, you could potentially earn more with your stocks than you will save by paying down your mortgage—though buying stocks does, of course, involve significantly more risk.

## Shifting the Burden

Paying down debt will reduce the interest you pay. But you can also cut your interest payments by consolidating your debts. The classic strategy: Use a mortgage to pay off other, higher-cost borrowing. We may not be considered as creditworthy as the federal government. But when we take out a mortgage, we're typically charged a relatively low interest rate, because the loan is backed by our home and thus lenders know they have an asset they can seize if we don't make our mortgage payments. In addition, mortgage interest may be tax-deductible—which isn't the case with the interest on most of our other debts, such as auto loans and credit cards. Sound like debt consolidation is just the ticket? Keep a couple of caveats in mind.

You could pay off other debts by refinancing your current home loan and taking out a larger mortgage. Alternatively, you might leave your current mortgage alone and instead pay off your other debts with a second mortgage, such as a home equity loan or line of credit. Whichever route you go, avoid turning this into a spending spree. The temptation: to borrow more than is needed to pay off your other debts and then use the extra cash to take a cruise or buy a new car.

If you decide to refinance your existing mortgage, don't just focus on the size of your new monthly mortgage payment. If you are, say, 12 years into paying down your 30-year mortgage, you might be able to refinance, take out a larger loan to eliminate your other debts, and still cut your monthly mortgage payments. This might seem like a neat trick. But unfortunately, in the process, you could be setting yourself back financially.

If you apply for another 30-year loan, you are taking what's now an 18-year mortgage and spreading the payments over 30 years. Not surprisingly, that can trim your monthly payment. But you are also signing up for an extra 12 years of indentured servitude to the mortgage company and that could have all kinds of financial ramifications, including forcing you to delay retirement. My advice:

If you are consolidating debts by refinancing, forget the 30-year mortgage—and see if you can afford the payments on a 15-year or 20-year loan instead.

---

### Street Smarts

- Got credit card debt? Paying it off could be one of the best investments you can make.
- If you're a conservative investor inclined to buy bonds, consider making extra principal payments on your mortgage instead.
- When consolidating debts, resist the temptation to borrow more so you can finance another spending spree.

---

# Chapter Seventeen

# Saving Taxes Can Cost Us Dearly

*But Retirement Accounts Are
the Big Exception*

Iᴛ's ᴛʜᴇ ᴛᴀxᴘᴀʏᴇʀ's ʟᴀᴍᴇɴᴛ: If only I had more deductions.

Be careful of what you wish for.

There are all kinds of ways to pad your Schedule A,
the federal tax form where you list your itemized deductions. You could give more to charity, pay more in state
and local taxes, cough up more mortgage interest, and incur
hefty medical expenses.

Giving to charity is a great idea. But what about everything else? Should you really be happy to have more tax deductions?

## Pocketing Less

The reality: Racking up a heap of medical expenses and mortgage interest is hardly reason to celebrate. Such deductions are costing you a lot more than they're costing Uncle Sam. If you are in the 28 percent federal income tax bracket, you itemize your deductions and you pay $1 of mortgage interest, you will save 28 cents in taxes—which means the other 72 cents is coming out of your pocket.

In addition, if you hadn't amassed all those money-losing tax deductions, you would still be entitled to the standard deduction. In 2009, the standard deduction is worth $11,400 to folks who are married filing jointly and $5,700 to those who are single. In effect, you are only truly saving taxes with that portion of your itemized deduction that exceeds the standard deduction that you could otherwise have taken.

To make matters worse, if you have a six-figure income, Uncle Sam may reduce your itemized deduction in 2009. If you're subject to the alternative minimum tax, it gets even more punishing. Under the AMT, some itemized deductions aren't allowed, including those for state and local taxes.

## Doubling Trouble

Among all the possible tax deductions, the deduction for mortgage interest seems to have a special grip on the public's imagination. It's deemed so valuable that some people think you should always have a mortgage. Long gone are old-fashioned notions about retiring debt-free. Lately, more seniors are carrying mortgage debt, possibly because they're convinced that all that mortgage interest is saving them a bundle in taxes. But in truth, this supposedly valuable tax deduction can wreak havoc with your total tax bill.

Once retired, you have to get the money to pay the mortgage from somewhere. Maybe you will sell winning investments in your taxable account. Maybe you will draw down your retirement accounts. Either way, that will mean additional taxable income. This extra taxable income may, in turn, cause up to 85 percent of your Social Security retirement benefit to be taxable. This tax on your Social Security kicks in when your income breaches certain thresholds. Result: Making those mortgage payments can trigger a double tax hit, first on your investment gains and then on Social Security.

To be sure, your mortgage interest may be tax deductible, and that will partially offset this double tax hit. But if you have had the mortgage for a while and paid down a fair amount of the loan, maybe less than half of your monthly payment will consist of interest, so you won't have much interest to deduct. You may even discover that you don't have enough deductions to make it worthwhile to itemize. That means you will instead take the standard deduction, which is available to everybody, including those who are mortgage-free. In that scenario, carrying a mortgage isn't saving you anything in taxes—but it may trigger a stinging tax bill by forcing you to tap retirement accounts or sell winning investments, while also unleashing taxes on your Social Security retirement benefit.

## Growing Free

That said, there is one tax deduction that is enormously valuable—and that's the deduction for retirement account contributions. With other deductions, you fork over $1 to somebody else and save maybe 28 cents in taxes. But with a 401(k) plan or a tax-deductible individual retirement account, you save the 28 cents in taxes, and you still have the dollar you invested.

Some argue that funding 401(k) plans and IRAs are setting folks up for big tax bills in retirement, because most or all of the money withdrawn will be taxable as ordinary income. But if you do the math, you discover that the initial tax deduction often pays for this eventual tax bill.

To understand why, suppose you contributed $1,000 to a 401(k). If you hadn't stashed the $1,000 in the 401(k), you would have immediately lost $280 to taxes, assuming you're in the 28 percent federal income tax bracket. That would leave you with just $720 to invest or spend. Indeed, when you look at your retirement account and you figure in the initial tax deduction, think of $720 as belonging to you and the other $280 as belonging to Uncle Sam.

Over the next two decades, imagine the $1,000 you stashed in the 401(k) triples in value to $3,000. You then pull out the money, paying 28 percent in taxes, equal to $840. That leaves you with $2,160 to spend. As it turns out, this $2,160 is triple the $720 you would have had, assuming you hadn't funded the 401(k). In effect, when you cashed out your 401(k), you simply repaid the initial tax deduction, leaving you with tax-free investment growth on the remaining money.

True, if your tax bracket turns out to be higher in retirement, you won't enjoy totally tax-free growth. Still, you will likely be far ahead of where you would have been if you had instead invested through a regular taxable account. You don't get a tax deduction for funding a taxable account, plus you have to pay taxes each year on any dividends, interest, and realized capital gains. Those taxes would slow the account's investment growth. You would also face taxes when you cashed out any remaining unrealized capital gains at the end of the two decades.

Moreover, there is a good chance your tax bracket will be lower in retirement. That may cut the tax bill when you sell your taxable account's investments and realize any remaining untaxed capital gains. But it would be especially good for your 401(k), allowing you to profit at the government's expense. Uncle Sam gave you the initial tax deduction when you were in a high tax bracket. But, when it comes time to cash out your 401(k) and return the favor, your tax bracket is lower—and Uncle Sam gets stiffed.

Not sure your tax bracket will be lower in retirement? You might instead fund a Roth IRA, if you're eligible, and also a Roth 401(k), if your employer offers one. With the Roth, there's no tax deduction for your contributions, but everything withdrawn in retirement is tax-free.

Given that a lot hinges on your individual situation, you might get a few pointers from your tax adviser, if you have one. Alternatively, you could simply hedge your bets, putting part of your money in regular tax-deductible retirement accounts and part in Roth accounts. That way, you will be in pretty good shape, no matter what happens to your tax bracket in retirement. Remember how you diversified your investments? Think of this as tax diversification.

## Street Smarts

- Strive to pay off your mortgage and other debts by retirement.
- Ignore the naysayers—and make the most of 401(k) and other retirement accounts.
- Diversify your tax exposure by funding both Roth and regular retirement accounts.

# Chapter Eighteen

# A Tax Deferred Is
# Extra Money Made

*Why We Should Keep
Uncle Sam Waiting*

O CCASIONALLY, PROCRASTINATION PAYS.

Much of the time, we're in a financial rush. The quicker we pay off our debts, the less interest we'll incur. The younger we start saving, the more we can potentially gain from investment compounding. The earlier we buy our first home, the sooner we can start building up home equity.

But when it comes to paying taxes on our investment gains, we should take it slow. If we can postpone paying Uncle Sam his share, we can use that money to notch additional investment gains—and that can give a big boost to our retirement nest egg.

## Delaying the Day

Consider a simple example. Let's say you are age 40, you're in the 25 percent federal income tax bracket, and you invest $1,000 that goes on to earn 8 percent a year. If you pay taxes on your entire gain every year, you would have $4,292 at age 65. But if you postpone taxes until age 65 and then pay the bill on your 25 years of tax-deferred growth, you would amass $5,386. As you would expect, the longer you can delay the day of tax reckoning, the larger the advantage. Take the same scenario, but this time assume you invest for 40 years. If you pay taxes every year, you would have $10,286 after four decades, versus $16,543 if you put off the tax bill until the end.

How can you postpone paying taxes? There are two ways. First, you could fund tax-deferred retirement accounts, such as 401(k) plans, individual retirement accounts, and variable annuities. The IRA might also give you an initial tax deduction. The 401(k) could be even sweeter, offering both an initial tax deduction and a matching employer contribution.

Second, you can hold off selling the winning investments you own in your taxable account. By hanging on to your winning taxable account investments for longer, you postpone the capital gains tax bill and you thus get to use the government's money for longer. This strategy runs counter to many folks' instincts. They like to sell their winners quickly, so they have the pleasure of turning their paper profits into cold cash. At the same time, they leave their losing investments alone, so there's a chance they will recoup their losses. But while selling winners and hanging on to losers may be more emotionally satisfying, it's bad for your tax bill. Not only are you realizing your gains quickly, but also you aren't taking advantage of your losses. On your federal tax return, those losses can be used to offset your capital gains and up to $3,000 of ordinary income each year.

That said, hanging on to winners could be a risky strategy if you have a lot of money riding on one or two stocks. In that situation, you may want to sell your winners, take the tax hit, and diversify more broadly. Better still, you might try sidestepping this dilemma, by steering clear of individual stocks and instead using your taxable account to buy mutual funds you can see holding for a good long time. Which funds fit that bill? You would want diversified, tax-efficient, low-cost funds whose fortunes don't hinge on the success of one or two fund managers.

That, of course, is pretty much the definition of an index fund, a subject we discussed in Chapter Ten.

## Splitting Up

As you aim to defer taxes for as long as possible, you will probably want to hold stocks in your taxable account and keep your bonds in your retirement account. This doesn't mean your retirement account money should be entirely in bonds and your taxable account money should be entirely in stocks. You shouldn't let your split of taxable money and retirement account money drive your stock-bond mix, which instead should depend on a host of other factors, including your time horizon and appetite for risk.

But, to the extent you own bonds, you should try to hold them in your retirement account. That way, you can defer the tax bill on the interest that your bonds kick off each year. In addition, you can use your retirement account to go for the extra return potentially offered by taxable bonds. By contrast, if you buy your bonds in your taxable account, you might favor lower-yielding municipal bonds, which kick off interest that is exempt from federal taxes and, in some cases, state and local taxes as well. Munis often make sense for taxable account investors in the 28 percent federal income tax bracket and higher.

Meanwhile, if you hold your stock index funds or other tax-efficient stock funds in your taxable account, your annual investment tax bill should be modest. Your stock funds may kick off dividends. But if your funds are tax-efficient, you shouldn't get much in the way of capital gains distributions each year. Instead, much of your capital gain will remain unrealized—which means there won't be a capital gains tax bill until you sell part or all of your fund holdings. As a bonus, both qualified dividends and realized long-term capital gains are currently taxed at a lower rate than ordinary income.

This advice will strike some folks as wrong-headed. They're more comfortable holding bonds in their taxable account. The reason: If they need money in a hurry, they figure they'll be in better shape if they have the option of selling bonds, which aren't subject to the wild price swings that afflict stocks. The problem is, if those bonds are sitting in a retirement account, getting at the money could spark income taxes and possible tax penalties.

But it is easy enough to get around this problem. Let's say you suddenly need $7,000 for a medical bill and all you have in your taxable account are stock funds, which are in the midst of getting mauled by a bear market. Nonetheless, to get cash, you sell $7,000 of stocks in your taxable account. That means you have just sold shares at bear market prices, which isn't exactly smart. To undo the damage, you simultaneously move $7,000 from bonds to stocks within your retirement account. This wouldn't trigger any sort of tax bill. What is the upshot of all this financial finagling? You have reduced your bonds by $7,000, kept the same stock exposure—and got the money you need for your medical expenses.

## Padding the Bill

While holding down your investment tax bill is usually a smart strategy, sometimes you'll want deliberately to realize a lot of gains if you find yourself in a year with very little taxable income. That could happen if you lost your job or you're early in your career. But it is also likely to occur early in retirement—and you may want to seize that opportunity.

Suppose you retire at age 60. You no longer have a paycheck and you haven't yet claimed Social Security. Instead, your only taxable income is the interest, dividends, and mutual fund distributions kicked off by your taxable-account investments. Indeed, there is a chance you will have a year or two when you owe nothing in taxes. That might seem like bliss. But in truth, it's a wasted opportunity.

After all, you could use those years to, say, sell winning stock positions in your taxable account or pull money out of your retirement accounts and, either way, pay very little in taxes. Alternatively, you might convert part of your regular IRA to a Roth IRA. You will have to pay income taxes on the taxable sum converted. But once the money is in your Roth, it will grow tax-free thereafter and, unlike with a regular IRA, you won't be compelled to pull money out of the account every year after you turn age 70 ½. It's especially smart to do this sort of tax management before you claim Social Security. Once you start Social Security, there is a risk that any extra investment income will trigger taxes on your Social Security benefit. That means you will end up paying taxes on both your extra investment income and Social Security, thus effectively suffering a double tax hit.

One possibility: Consider slating the first three or four years of your retirement for some tax management. During those initial retirement years, hold off claiming Social Security and instead use the time to sell winning taxable-account investments, draw down your IRA, or convert part of your IRA to a Roth. You might even build up a cash kitty during your final working years, to cover the tax bill on the investment gains you generate during this stretch.

How much extra investment income should you aim to generate during these years? If you use a tax adviser, your adviser should be able to do the calculation for you, taking into account your individual situation. But suppose that, once you become age 70 ½ and start taking required minimum distributions from your retirement accounts, you figure you will be in the 25 percent federal income tax bracket. Many retirees are surprised by how much they end up paying in taxes in their seventies and eighties, once those required retirement account distributions kick in. To cut down on the amount of income that ends up getting taxed at that rate, you might aim to generate sufficient income each year in your sixties to get to the top of the 15 percent federal income tax bracket.

Let's assume you are single and, on your tax return, you take one personal exemption and the standard deduction. If you are under age 65, you could have $43,300 in total income in 2009 and still remain within the 15 percent tax bracket. If you are age 65 or older, your standard deduction would be slightly higher. Similarly, if you are married and take the standard deduction and two personal exemptions, you could go as high as $86,600 and still stay within the 15 percent tax bracket. Deliberately paying taxes at 15 percent may not sound so great. But it sure beats paying taxes at 25 percent just a few years later.

---

### Street Smarts

- Get tax-deferred growth by funding retirement accounts and hanging on to winning investments in your taxable account.
- Hold bonds in your retirement accounts and keep stocks in your taxable account.
- If you have a year with little or no taxable income, consider deliberately realizing investment gains.

## Chapter Nineteen

# Insurance Won't Make Us Any Money—If We're Lucky

~

### *The Best Protection Is a Plump Portfolio*

COLLECTING ON AN INSURANCE POLICY? So sorry to hear it.

After all, if you're collecting, that usually means something unfortunate has happened—a car crash, a disability, a hospital stay. What if nothing truly unfortunate has happened and you are getting a check from the insurance company? That is a sign you may be buying too much insurance coverage.

Insurance is a way to get somebody else to shoulder financial risks that we can't afford to shoulder ourselves, things like the house burning down or the family's main breadwinner dying. But this isn't the approach many people take. They use insurance to protect against minor risks and they endeavor to turn it into a moneymaker—and that leads to all kinds of foolishness.

## Taking Cover

What foolishness? People purchase unnecessary coverage, they buy policies with low deductibles, and they try to make insurance an investment. Let's take each of those three in turn.

First, there are those small risks, things like our appliances going into meltdown or having to cancel the family vacation at the last minute. Yes, it is upsetting when the washing machine or the stereo head off to the electronics' graveyard. But in all likelihood, we can afford to replace them, so it hardly constitutes the sort of devastating financial risk that we need others to shoulder. The implication: Forget the extended warranty that the salesperson tries to get you to buy, right after he or she has told you how wonderful the product is. Similarly, skip the trip cancellation insurance that the travel agent pushes so relentlessly. It might be distressing to cancel the cruise and lose much or all of the money you paid—but it probably wouldn't be a financial disaster.

Second, to boost the likelihood that their insurance will pay off, folks will keep the deductibles low on their auto, health, and homeowner's insurance. They will also buy disability and long-term care policies that have a short waiting period before benefits kick in. But the odds are, you can afford to pay the first $1,000 needed to fix the fender bender and you can find some way to cover costs during the initial 180 days that you are disabled.

Indeed, in trying to increase the chance that their insurance policies will pay off, people may leave themselves exposed to far bigger risks. Take long-term care insurance, one of the costlier policies out there. Folks will buy policies where they have to wait only a brief period before benefits kick in. But this short elimination period drives up the policy's premium, so buyers might also opt for a policy that pays just three years of benefits.

Yet this totally misses what the real danger is. The big risk isn't being in a nursing home for six months or a year. Rather, the big risk is being in a nursing home for a decade or longer. That is what you really need insurance for. You could likely find some way to pay for the first six months or a year. But if you ended up in a nursing home for 10 years, you might blow through all your savings and end up on Medicaid. To figure out what your best option is, ask your insurance agent to get quotes for a fistful of policies with different elimination periods and different benefit amounts, so that you can see the tradeoffs involved.

Third, people try to ensure their life insurance is a moneymaker by purchasing cash-value life insurance. Life insurance policies can be divided into two camps, cash value and term. Term policies provide a death benefit—and that's it. If you don't die during the term of the policy, you won't have anything to show for your premium dollars. By contrast, cash-value policies offer not only a death benefit, but also the chance to build up cash value by having part of your annual premium invested in a tax-deferred account. Result: If you surrender the policy, you should get at least some money back. Indeed, cash-value life insurance is one insurance policy where you really should hope to make money.

The problem is, the annual premium on cash-value life insurance is typically far higher than the premium on a term policy with the same benefit. As a result, there is a danger buyers will skimp on coverage if they opt for the cash-value policy, which means their family could be in financial trouble if they die prematurely. In addition, cash-value policies just aren't a great way to get tax-deferred growth, because these policies typically involve high costs.

Many people can get tax deferral more cheaply through their 401(k) and their individual retirement account. Unlike with a cash-value policy, you should also get an immediate tax deduction when you stash dollars in your 401(k) and you might receive a matching contribution from your employer. Similarly, funding an IRA may garner you an immediate tax deduction.

## Assuming Risk

Fans of cash-value life insurance will note that, while the premium on a cash-value policy should remain constant, the cost of term insurance can skyrocket as folks grow older. And that's true. But as you grow older, your children will likely leave home and you should accumulate some savings. That means you may not need life insurance. You no longer have financial dependents—and, if you do, you have some savings to bequeath to them if you die prematurely.

This brings up a key point: The best way to cut your insurance costs is to amass a decent amount of savings, so that you need less insurance. Recall the virtuous cycle described in Chapter Five. If you start saving as soon as you enter the workforce and you quickly amass a decent amount of savings, your wealth will allow you to trim all kinds of living expenses, including your insurance.

On that score, consider again my suggestion that you eschew extended warranties, raise the deductibles on your auto, health, and homeowner's policies and opt for longer waiting periods on your disability and long-term care insurance. It is a lot easier to stomach all of this if you have some savings, a plan for dealing with financial emergencies, and your living expenses are under control. For instance, let's say you are purchasing a disability policy and you are wondering what sort of waiting period you should opt for.

Selecting a long elimination period can be a pretty easy decision if your spouse works, because you might be able to get by on your spouse's income if you can't work. What if you are single or your spouse doesn't pull in a paycheck? It will be less risky to buy a policy with a long waiting period if you have some savings in your regular taxable account that you can fall back on. You might even build up a separate emergency reserve, equal to maybe three or six months of living expenses.

Alternatively, you could line up various ways to borrow money in a financial emergency. For example, you might have a home equity line of credit or you might hold your tax-able-account investments in a margin account, so you can borrow against their value. Because of the risk involved in borrowing on margin, consider limiting your margin loans to 20 percent or less of your investment account's value.

Finally, give yourself some financial flexibility by keep-ing core living expenses to 50 percent or less of pretax income. These core living expenses include items like mortgage or rent, utilities, food, and insurance. That leaves the other 50 percent for entertainment, savings, and taxes. If you crashed the car or you couldn't work because of an accident, it would be a lot easier to cope financially if you have your monthly costs firmly under control. While you cover the tab for the car repair, you could trim your savings rate and cut back on entertainment. And if you couldn't work because of an accident, your income tax bill would also go way down. Indeed, if you had to, you could get by on just half of your old salary. That knowledge should give you some financial peace of mind—and the courage to reduce your insurance coverage.

## Street Smarts

- Don't pay an insurance company to shoulder risks you can afford to shoulder yourself.
- To cut your insurance costs, raise deductibles and extend elimination periods.
- If you don't have financial dependents, you probably don't need life insurance.

*Chapter Twenty*

# Even If We Have a Will, We May Not Get Our Way

~

*Don't Fret Over Estate Taxes—but Worry About Those Legal Bills*

LET THE PAPER CHASE BEGIN.

To ensure that your money ends up with your loved ones, you need a will. But you also need a whole lot more than that—because there is a good chance your will won't determine who gets the bulk of your estate.

Imagine a fairly typical situation. You are married. You own your home jointly with your spouse. You have a life insurance policy. You have money in a 401(k) plan and an individual retirement account. And, when it comes to things of real financial value, that's pretty much it. So who gets your money when you die? Don't bother reading your will.

## Dodging Probate

Your will governs those assets that pass through the probate courts. Those courts oversee the settling of your estate, including confirming that your will is valid, making sure your debts are paid, and ensuring your final wishes are carried out. But many assets don't pass through probate. For instance, if you and your spouse own a home jointly with right of survivorship, it will go directly to your spouse if you die first. Similarly, your 401(k) and IRA will typically be inherited by the beneficiaries named on those accounts, and your life insurance proceeds will usually pass to the beneficiaries listed on the policy. What if you never updated the beneficiaries on your life insurance and it still lists your ex-husband? There's a good chance he'll get the last laugh.

Meanwhile, if you place assets in a trust before you die, they will be inherited by the trust's beneficiaries. Some people use a living trust to hold their assets so that, upon their death, their assets pass directly to the named beneficiaries, rather than going through probate. By placing assets in a living trust, you avoid the publicity that review by the probate court can entail. More important, a living trust can save on legal costs, assuming probate in your state is a costly process. A living trust can make particular sense if you own a vacation home in another state. By putting the vacation home in a living trust, you sidestep the necessity for your estate to go through probate in two states.

On the other hand, if probate is no great hassle in the state where you reside, setting up a living trust may wind up boosting your overall legal bill, rather than reducing it. Indeed, living trusts can be oversold. Contrary to what is sometimes claimed, a living trust alone won't cut your estate tax bill. In other words, if you put assets in a living trust and they pass outside of the probate court, they could still be subject to estate taxes. Avoiding probate and avoiding estate taxes aren't the same thing.

## Cleaning Up

That doesn't mean you can't use trusts to cut your estate tax bill. For example, if a husband and wife are fairly wealthy, they might use something called a bypass trust. A husband and wife can leave unlimited sums to each other tax-free. But money left to other folks could be subject to estate taxes, assuming the total sum involved is above the federal estate tax exemption, which in 2009 is $3.5 million. The problem: If the first spouse to die bequeaths everything to the surviving spouse, the assets will pass free of estate taxes—but the first spouse's estate tax exemption is effectively wasted.

This isn't a big deal, unless you and your spouse are together worth more than $3.5 million, in which case you will want to make sure you both use your federal estate tax exemption. That is where the bypass trust comes in. Let's say you died first. At that juncture, up to $3.5 million would flow into a trust with, say, your children named as beneficiaries but with your spouse still able to use the money. That uses your $3.5 million exemption. When your spouse dies, another $3.5 million would also pass free of federal estate taxes, assuming the estate tax exemption remains at 2009's level. Result: You have avoided estate taxes on $7 million.

There's a good chance you are reading this and thinking, "That's all very interesting, but it sure doesn't apply to me, because I don't have anything like $3.5 million, yet alone $7 million." And you are not alone. Federal estate taxes aren't an issue for perhaps 99 percent of U.S. citizens. Despite all the hand-wringing over the "death tax," it just isn't something most of us need to worry about.

One caveat: Estate taxes levied by your state may kick in at a far lower asset level.

Instead, the big cost triggered by your death is likely to be legal costs. That is why a living trust may make sense, assuming probate is arduous in your state or you own out-of-state property. But there are also other, much simpler things you can do to ensure your death doesn't end up enriching the local legal community.

Like what? By all means, get a will to cover those assets that pass through probate. But don't stop there. As you might have gathered, there's a bunch of other paperwork involved. Check that you have the right beneficiaries listed on your life insurance and your retirement accounts. See if you have the ownership of your home structured the right way. Draft a letter of instructions, specifying what sort of funeral you want, where key documents are located, and who should get your personal effects. Be warned: A letter of instructions is not a substitute for a will.

In addition, consider drawing up a living will that specifies your wishes concerning life-prolonging medical procedures. You might also want a health care power of attorney that names somebody to make medical decisions on your behalf and a durable power of attorney that appoints somebody to make financial decisions for you should you become incapacitated. The older you are, the more critical it is to have these legal documents.

Finally, make sure your financial affairs are well organized and talk to your family about what they can expect from your estate. That conversation is particularly important if you are distributing your assets unevenly by, say, favoring one child over another. If your family has a good idea of what they will receive from your estate, they are less likely to contest your will and fight over your assets. With those sorts of fights, everybody loses—except, of course, the lawyers.

---

### Street Smarts

- Get a will to cover those assets that pass through probate.
- Make sure you have the right beneficiaries listed on your life insurance and retirement accounts.
- Talk to your family about what they can expect from your estate.

# Chapter Twenty-One

# Financial Success: It's About More Than Money

~

*Family Can Be Our Greatest Asset—and Our Greatest Liability*

WHAT'S THE KEY TO GETTING RICH? If you think it is beating the market or earning a fat salary, think again.

Yes, higher investment returns will help you accumulate the money needed for the house down payment, the kids' college education, and your own retirement. Yes, if you're hauling in a hefty paycheck, you should find it easier to amass a decent-size nest egg.

But these are just two of the factors that propel your nest egg's growth—and they aren't necessarily the most important.

## Playing Parent

So what is important? High up on the list is family, which can have a huge impact on our finances, sometimes in ways we don't even realize.

Clearly, if we have wealthy parents, we might get a high-priced education that sets us up for a high-paying job. We might also graduate debt-free, enjoy regular parental handouts, and one day inherit a handsome sum. But even without that sort of financial assistance, family can make a big difference. For instance, if we are close with our parents and with our siblings and we know they would help out if we got into financial trouble, we may be more inclined to take risk. That might mean skimping on insurance, favoring stocks over bonds, and funding the 401(k) rather than building up the big emergency reserve. All of that could mean more wealth.

Getting married can also have a major impact on our finances. Two people together can live more cheaply than two people living separately. But those cost savings go out the window with the arrival of children. Not only does starting a family mean extra expenses, but also it may prompt one parent to quit work and stay home instead to raise the kids. Don't take this as an argument for not having children. I have two of them, expenses by the name of Hannah and Henry, and I wouldn't trade them for anything. But we also shouldn't delude ourselves: Kids aren't cheap—and, if we have them, we will likely retire later. When I was at the *Wall Street Journal,* I would often receive e-mails from readers boasting of how they had managed to retire in their forties. I would then write back and ask whether they had children. Invariably, the answer was "no."

According to the U.S. Department of Agriculture, it costs more than $200,000 for a middle-income family to raise a child through to his eighteenth birthday. Parents then have college costs on top of that. Today, that can mean forking over another $200,000 if the child goes to an elite private institution. Moreover, the cost of kids is increasingly extending beyond the undergraduate years, as children go on to get graduate degrees, spend their initial working years in unpaid internships, and live at home after college.

Finally have an empty nest? If we also hope to sever the financial apron strings, we need to lay the groundwork years earlier. The goal: Raise money-smart kids who know how to live within their means. That isn't easy. Children grow up spending their parents' money, so they don't have much incentive to limit their desires. The trick is to get kids to feel like they are spending their own money by, for instance, giving them an allowance and then forcing them to live within that budget. It helps if parents regularly discuss financial issues, including how to invest sensibly and the importance of paying off credit cards in full. Parents should also talk about their own financial struggles when they first entered the workforce, so kids are prepared for lean times when they're in their twenties.

Even if children grow up to be financially responsible adults, parents may find they aren't completely off the hook. When kids buy their first home, mom and dad often cough up part of the down payment. When children get married, parents frequently foot the bill.

Weddings, of course, are happy occasions. But, unfortunately, these things can also go into reverse. If we want to lose half of our wealth, we could invest heavily in stocks just ahead of a brutal bear market—or we could get divorced. I am not suggesting that folks should stay in an unhappy marriage for the sake of their finances. But people could save themselves a lot of financial grief if they were slower to tie the knot—and slower to untie it.

While children may be costly, parents can also carry a price tag. Suppose our elderly parents are ailing and need assistance with daily living activities. If they have a heap of money, they could pay for visiting nurses, a cleaning service, and other home help. But if our parents aren't well-heeled, there is a chance they are headed for the nursing home—unless their adult children pitch in. Faced with that choice, kids may scale back the hours they work or even quit their jobs entirely, so they can help their elderly parents.

## Losing with Style

Like family, lifestyle choices can have a crucial influence on our wealth. There's the obvious impact: If we are big spenders, we will save less and we'll need a larger nest egg to sustain the same lifestyle in retirement. That might necessitate delaying retirement, while we amass more money, and even then we may have to cut back our standard of living once we quit the workforce.

We associate wealth with the trappings of wealth, including the designer clothes and the luxury cars. But these trappings aren't a sign of wealth. Rather, they are a sign of money spent—and the people involved are poorer for it. In fact, the richest family in the neighborhood may live in the smallest house with the oldest cars. Their frugality allows them to save like crazy. I am not suggesting this is desirable. Neither spendthrifts nor misers deserve our admiration. Instead, we should strive to strike the right balance, spending our money on the things that are important to us, but also saving enough for our goals.

Our lifestyle choices aren't just about spending. There are also health issues. If we smoke two packs a day, drink heavily, and never exercise, we may struggle with our health, limit our ability to work, and incur hefty medical bills. We will likely also shorten our life expectancy, so maybe we don't need to fund such a long retirement. But that, I suspect, will be scant consolation.

## Getting Lucky

Even if we are careful, we may be on the losing end of the genetic lottery and find ourselves battling medical problems. Alternatively, maybe our spouse or one of the children will suffer ill health. Once again, that might limit our ability to work and it might mean large medical and other bills. That brings us to the final factor, luck, which is an issue not only with our health, but also with our careers.

We like to think that if we work hard, we will get ahead in our jobs. But sometimes, life doesn't work out that way. Maybe our adopted career is in an industry that is struggling and our efforts to save are interrupted by occasional bouts of unemployment. Similarly, maybe we have a set of skills that isn't in great demand. We hear about hedge-fund managers who amass millions and even billions of dollars. These folks have talents that are highly valued in today's economy. But someone with the same set of skills living in a different time or a different country might not be nearly so valued—and they might rank as a humble member of the middle class.

What's the lesson here? There are factors we have little or no control over, like whether our employer gets into financial trouble or whether our parents are wealthy or poor. But there are also factors that we can control, like our spending habits, whether we look after our health, and whether we endeavor to raise money-smart kids. It's sort of like investing. We can't control how the markets perform. But we have a fair amount of control over how much we save, how much risk we take, and how much we incur in investment costs.

The implication: We shouldn't feel badly about the things we can't control—and we should focus on the things we can. We may never earn the six-figure income and we may never have the seven-figure portfolio. But we can still achieve that sense that we're in charge of our financial life and we can still squeeze a heap of happiness out of the dollars we have.

### Street Smarts

- Try to raise money-savvy kids by regularly discussing financial issues, recounting your own struggles, and putting your children on an allowance and leaving them to budget the money.
- Look after your health, so you last almost as long as your savings.
- A fat paycheck and a hefty portfolio would be nice—but you can achieve financial peace of mind without them.

# Conclusion

~

## *Wall Street? That Isn't So Far from Main Street*

For far too many people, managing money is confined to an occasional hour at the weekend, when they balance their checkbook, pay the bills, and review their mutual fund statements. But if we cordon off our finances like this, we're passing up the chance to get so much more out of our money.

As I hope you have gathered from the preceding pages, money is inextricably entwined with the rest of our lives. Yes, if Wall Street is viewed as the stock market, the brokerage firms, and the mutual fund companies, it is indeed a distinct entity. But if Wall Street is defined as the world of money, it's inseparable from Main Street.

Every decision we make—whether we buy the new coat, whether we go to the gym, whether we get married—has a financial impact.

This doesn't mean we should pause before every decision to contemplate its ramifications for our financial future. But it does mean we should make sure our money and the rest of our lives are aligned—and that means thinking much harder about how we spend our time and how we spend our money. Consider seven examples.

1. If our goal is to have more time with family, maybe we should ditch the high-spending lifestyle and go for the smaller house closer to work, so we don't have to fret so much about getting that next pay raise and we don't have to commute so far to the office.

2. If what we really want is to quit our jobs and do something more fulfilling but less lucrative, we should probably stop seeking salvation at the shopping mall—and start saving like crazy.

3. If our jobs aren't so secure, perhaps we shouldn't take on the big mortgage and maybe we shouldn't invest 100 percent in stocks.

4. If we are fearful that our family couldn't cope without us, maybe it is time to get a will, buy some life insurance, and check that we have the right beneficiaries on our retirement accounts.

5. If we are saving diligently for a 30-year retirement, we might also want to spend some time looking after our health, so our bodies last almost as long.

6. If the last bear market gave us ulcers and caused us sleepless nights, we may want to resist the impulse to invest heavily in stocks when the next bull market rolls around.

7. If we have alarming credit card debts and we can't recall where the money went, perhaps it is time to rethink how much we spend—and how we spend it.

The bottom line: We should strive to ensure money is enhancing our lives, rather than getting in the way. I'm not saying this is easy. Turbulent markets can prompt us to make panicky decisions. Impulse purchases can derail our plans to save. Worries about status can prod us to buy too big a home and too costly a car.

But if emotions can lead us astray, a little common sense can keep us on track. Let's face it, we know we can't spend our way to wealth. We have nagging doubts that the big house, with the huge mortgage and hefty utilities, will make us a fortune. We realize that owning a fancy car doesn't mean we're rich. We have a sneaking suspicion that the investment, which sounds too good to be true, probably is.

After 2008 and 2009's financial battering, it's time to give up on wishful thinking and supposedly miraculous solutions, and focus instead on a few simple truths. No, we won't get rich overnight. But if we're thoughtful about how we manage our money, we could grow wealthy over time—and, maybe more important, we'll have some financial peace of mind along the way.

# Acknowledgments

IF YOU LEARNED A LOT FROM THIS BOOK, don't thank me. Rather, thank my readers and sources, who have provided me with a wonderful financial education. Over the past quarter-century, many academics and many financial advisers have generously shared their time and their ideas with me—and many readers have called and written, telling me which of those ideas make sense.

My appreciation goes to colleagues Andy Sieg and Karen Damley, who championed this book, and to Jeff Fahs, David Glotzer, Alex Samuelson, and especially Ian Sandler, who took on the tedious task of reviewing the manuscript. What can I say? No pain, no gain.

Thanks also go to Wiley's Pamela van Giessen and Emilie Herman for their enthusiasm and their many ideas. This is the third book I've worked on with my incomparable agent, Wes Neff, and he once again delivered, offering his usual wry humor along the way.

I love writing. To me, there's something profoundly relaxing and satisfying about ripping off a first draft and then working and reworking the material, striving to polish the paragraphs and make the sentences sing. Indeed, writing is among my favorite activities, ranking right up there with drinking coffee in the early morning, running in the rain, bicycling at reckless speeds, napping after lunch, dining out with friends and sipping wine late at night.

But while these other activities can be done with others, writing is a solitary endeavor. Maybe that's why authors often heap thanks on their family. Time devoted to the book inevitably means time away from loved ones. Yes, sweet Carolyn, I know I'm ignoring you as I write these words. But that doesn't mean you aren't in my thoughts—and this book is for you.